INLG 2016 Workshop on Computational Creativity in Natural Language Generation (CC-NLG 2016)

Edinburgh, United Kingdom
5 September 2016

ISBN: 978-1-5108-3184-1

Introduction

Welcome to the INLG 2016 Workshop on Computational Creativity in Natural Language Generation. This workshop aims to bring together researchers dealing with text generation from a computational creativity perspective, and researchers in natural language generation with an interest in creative aspects. These two communities have been working separately for many years, as the focus in each one of them has been different: creativity research tends to be less focused on technical issues in natural language generation, and more on issues related to cognition, aesthetics, and novelty; while NLG research tends to focus on technical and theoretical aspects of processes, and information content and readability of output. However, recent progress in both fields is reducing many of these differences with creativity projects moving more towards robust implementation, and NLG research including stylistics, variation and literary genres such as poetry or narrative and we believe they are approaching the point where they can mutually benefit from ongoing work. By encouraging members of both communities to discuss work in related topics with each other, we hope to move towards better joint understanding of the problems involved.

Matthew Purver, Pablo Gervás and Sascha Griffiths

Workshop Chairs:

Matthew Purver, Queen Mary University of London
Pablo Gervás, Universidad Complutense de Madrid
Sascha Griffiths, Universität Hamburg

Program Committee:

David Elson, Google
Mark Granroth-Wilding, University of Cambridge
Cyril Labbé, Grenoble University
Carlos León, Universidad Complutense de Madrid
Maria Teresa Llano Rodriguez, Goldsmiths, University of London
Stephen McGregor, Queen Mary University of London
François Portet, Université Grenoble Alpes
Ehud Reiter, University of Aberdeen
Advaith Siddharthan, University of Aberdeen
Hannu Toivonen, University of Helsinki
Alessandro Valitutti, University College Dublin
Pierre-Luc Vaudry, Université de Montréal
Tony Veale, University College Dublin
Geraint Wiggins, Queen Mary University of London

Table of Contents

This page intentionally left blank.

Conference Programme

Monday 5th September

08:30–09:00   Registration

09:00–10:15 Session 1 (full presentations)

09:00–09:25   *Assembling Narratives with Associative Threads*
Pierre-Luc Vaudry and Guy Lapalme

09:25–09:50   *Human-like Natural Language Generation Using Monte Carlo Tree Search*
Kaori Kumagai, Ichiro Kobayashi, Daichi Mochihashi, Hideki Asoh, Tomoaki Nakamura and Takayuki Nagai

09:50–10:15   *Empirical Determination of Basic Heuristics for Narrative Content Planning*
Pablo Gervás

10:15–10:30   Coffee

10:30–11:30 Session 2 (short presentations)

10:30–10:45   *X575: Writing Rengas with Web Services*
Daniel Winterstein and Joseph Corneli

10:45–11:00   *A Challenge to the Third Hoshi Shinichi Award*
Satoshi Sato

11:00–11:15   *Automatic Modification of Communication Style in Dialogue Management*
Louisa Pragst, Juliana Miehle, Stefan Ultes and Wolfgang Minker

11:15–11:30   *Mining Knowledge in Storytelling Systems for Narrative Generation*
Eugenio Concepción, Pablo Gervás and Gonzalo Méndez

11:30–11:40   Quick breath of fresh air

11:40–12:30 Session 3 (full presentations)

11:40–12:05   *Process Based Evaluation of Computer Generated Poetry*
Stephen McGregor, Matthew Purver and Geraint Wiggins

12:05–12:30   *Combinatorics vs Grammar: Archeology of Computational Poetry in Tape Mark I*
Alessandro Mazzei and Andrea Valle

12:30   Close & lunch

Assembling Narratives with Associative Threads

Pierre-Luc Vaudry and **Guy Lapalme**
RALI-DIRO – Université de Montréal
C.P. 6128, succ. Centre-Ville
Montréal, QC, Canada H3C 3J8
`{vaudrypl,lapalme}@iro.umontreal.ca`

Abstract

A model is proposed showing how automatically extracted and manually written association rules can be used to build the structure of a narrative from real-life temporal data. The generated text's communicative goal is to help the reader construct a causal representation of the events. A connecting associative thread allows the reader to follow associations from the beginning to the end of the text. It is created using a spanning tree over a selected associative sub-network. The results of a text quality evaluation show that the texts were understandable, but that flow between sentences, although not bad, could still be improved.

1   Introduction

A narrative is a text presenting with a certain angle a series of logically and chronologically related events caused or experienced by actors (Bal, 2009, p. 5). A data-to-text system summarizing temporal data including actions or activities should aim at generating such a text, if that corresponds to its users' needs. Some have pointed at causal relations as a means of improving the narrative aspect of temporal data-to-text (Hunter et al., 2012; Gervás, 2014).

The concepts of causal network and causal chain have been used to explain the process of narrative comprehension in humans (Trabasso and van Den Broek, 1985; Trabasso et al., 1989). Those causal networks are essentially composed of physical and mental events and states (of which goals and actions) connected by causal relations. Restrictions apply on which types of causal relation can

connect which types of event or state. The causal chain comprises the events that are on a path traversing the causal network from the introduction of the protagonists and setting to either goal attainment or the consequences of failure. Being on a causal chain and having more causal connections have both been found to increase chances of an event being recalled, included in a summary or judged important by the reader.

Swartjes and Theune (2006) and Theune et al. (2007) applied causal networks to the automatic creation of fairy tales. Several narrative data-to-text systems already identify and make use of some causal relations (Hallett, 2008; Hunter et al., 2012; Wanner et al., 2010; Bouayad-Agha et al., 2012). Going further, in Vaudry and Lapalme (2015) we have tried to extract a form of causal network from temporal data and use it to build the structure of the generated narrative. We used data mining techniques to extract sequential association rules and interpreted them as indicating potential, approximate causal relations. The resulting causal network was used to express locally some rhetorical relations in the sense of the Rhetorical Structure Theory (RST) (Mann and Thompson, 1987). However we did not succeed at exploiting it to build a complete rhetorical structure that would give the text a global coherence.

Building on what was begun, this paper proposes a model showing how automatically extracted and manually written association rules can be used to build the entire structure of a narrative from real-life temporal data.

In the course of our research, we found that it was very difficult to infer even the direction of a

Proceedings of the INLG 2016 Workshop on Computational Creativity and Natural Language Generation, pages 1–10,
Edinburgh, September 2016. ©2016 Association for Computational Linguistics

potential causal relation from an extracted association (see Section 4). If even that could not be determined, how could we claim to identify causal relations? We prefer to simply name *associations* the relations found during data interpretation. The task of inferring causal relations is left to the human reader of the generated text.

By association, we mean a connection between events or states without specifying the nature of the underlying relation. For example, an association can be based on a frequent sequence or a formal similarity. For the purpose of narrative comprehension, we assume that interesting associations are those that can help formulate causal hypotheses.

Note that although this is not a model for creating fictional narratives, its function is to suggest new associations between previously unassociated events. In this sense and to the extent that it accomplishes this, it can be considered to produce original, creative text (Jordanous, 2012, p. 257).

The proposed model assumes that the human reader can follow an associative thread from the beginning to the end of the text. The associations expressed between some of the events can give him hints toward building a mental representation of the events. His world and domain knowledge can enable him to sort through the expressed associations to retain and enrich the relevant ones. This can lead him to fill the gaps left by the text towards a causal interpretation of the events.

Section 2 presents our model of assisted temporal data interpretation. Section 3 presents the results of our efforts so far to evaluate this model. Related work is discussed in Section 4.

2   Model

This section presents our model of assisted temporal data interpretation using narrative generation. Figure 1 gives an overview of this model. We will refer to its components by using numbers for steps and letters for representation levels. Association rules come from two sources: data mining (1) for sequential association rules (B) from training data (A) and world and domain knowledge (C) formalized as rules (D). The data about a specific period (E) is interpreted (2) using the association rules to create an associative network (F). Then a sub-network containing the most unusual facts (G) is selected (3) using the probabilities of the corresponding sequential association rules (B). The following step of document structuring (4) involves determining the connecting associative thread going from the beginning to the end of the narrative (H). Microplanning (5) produces from this the lexico-syntactic specification (I). This specification is then realized (6) as a text (J) read by a human (7). The human reader uses his knowledge (C) to reason about the associations expressed in the text. From this he forms a mental representation which hypothetically includes a form of causal network (K). The following subsections detail each of these steps.

The communicative goal of the generated text in the context of this model is to communicate effectively the facts necessary to facilitate the construction of a causal network by the reader. By necessary facts, we mean the least easily predictable facts. Those facts are the most unusual (or least usual) of the summarized period compared to a typical period of the same kind of data. They are what makes this period unique. The associations expressed in the generated text should give valuable hints to the reader in constructing a causal mental representation of the events. Moreover, they should generally help see the events of the period as a coherent whole if such coherence can be found. This should help the reader assimilate effectively the text's content.

The facts not mentioned in the text should be implicitly understood as "same as usual" and the reader should be able to infer them approximately from the text's content if needed. According to Niehaus and Young (2014), the reader will make such an inference if it is necessary to the comprehension of the text (because of a break in a causal chain, for example) and not too difficult to make. The knowledge that the reader has of what usually happens, if the sequential association rules model that correctly enough, should enable the reader to make such inferences. In the case of the inferences that could be triggered in the reader by the expressed associations, it is much more difficult to use the criteria of necessity and enabledness, as exactly what should be inferred or not is not known by the computer.

To illustrate the various representation levels of the model, an example in the Activity of Daily Living (ADL) domain is provided in Figures 2, 3, 4, and

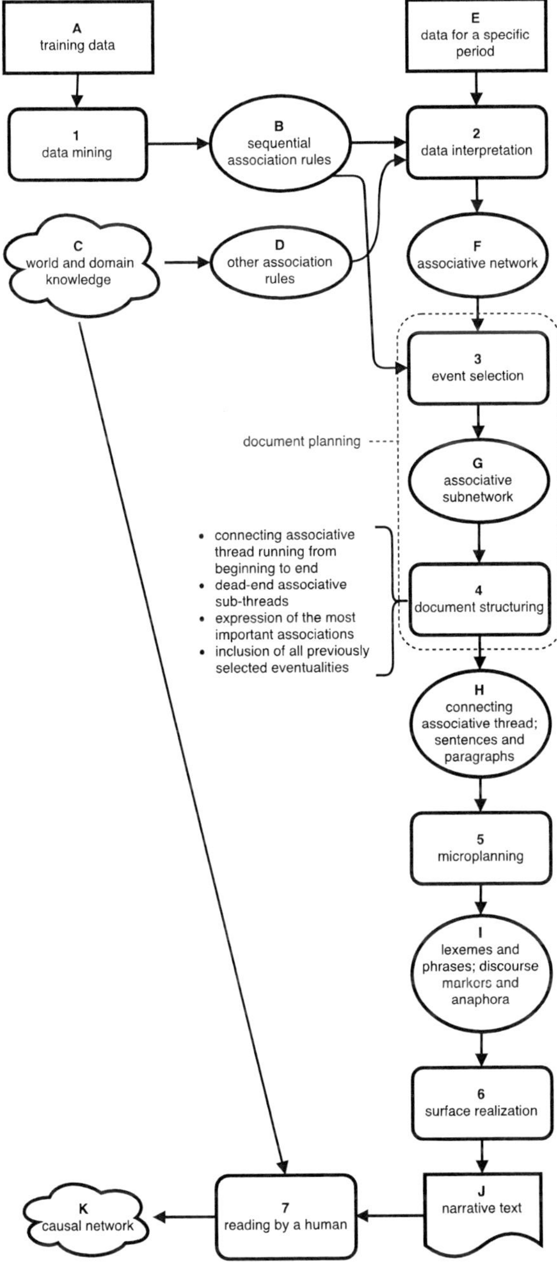

Figure 1: Assisted temporal data interpretation model. Rectangles represent input data; rounded rectangles: computational representations; ellipses: steps; clouds: hypothesized mental representations; rectangle with S-shaped bottom side: natural language document. For ease of reference, steps are identified by a number and representations by a letter.

5. The data it is based on is taken from the publicly available UCI ADL Binary Dataset (Ordóñez et al., 2013). This dataset contains 14 and 21 consecutive days of ADL data for users A and B, respectively. The data for each ADL occurrence consists of: start time, end time and activity label. The ADL label set is: *Sleeping, Toileting, Grooming, Showering, Breakfast, Lunch, Dinner, Snack, Spare_Time/TV, Leaving.* The input for this example consists of the data for user B as training data (A) and the portion covering the day of November 24, 2012 as the data to summarize (E).

2.1 Association Rules

Sequential Association Rule Mining: In step 1 on Figure 1, data mining techniques are used to select candidate sequential association rules based on confidence and significance. Confidence (cf in Figure 2) is computed as the conditional probability of encountering an instance of the rule given that the left side has been encountered. Depending on the confidence, associations are considered expected or unexpected. In the example, expected association rule candidates had $cf > 0.2$ and unexpected association rule candidates had $cf < 0.07$. This is roughly justified by the fact that since there are 10 activity types, the prior probability of one happening at any place in the sequence is 0.1. Significance measures the chances of the left and right sides of the rule of actually being independent according to the binomial distribution. In Figure 2, the p-values according to this distribution are called $p_{expected}$ and $p_{unexpected}$ for expected and unexpected association rules, respectively. In the example, a p-value lower than 0.05 was considered significant.

A rule can express a backward prediction. The chronological direction of each association rule is determined by computing the confidence for the two possible directions (chronological and reverse chronological) and retaining the direction with the highest one. That means that for candidate association AB, we checked which we could predict with more confidence: that B follows A or that A precedes B. This enabled us to better estimate the unusualness of each fact and thus improve content selection.

Rules 1 to 5 of Figure 2 are examples of mined sequential association rules.

Mined sequential association rules:

1. $H_{11,p} \rightarrow A_{Grooming,p}$
   $cf = 0.67, p_{expected} = 0.000005$

2. $A_{Sleeping,p-1} \leftarrow A_{Breakfast,p}$
   $cf = 0.23, p_{expected} = 0.01$

3. $A_{Showering,p-2} \rightarrow A_{Grooming,p}$
   $cf = 0.64, p_{expected} = 0.01$

4. $A_{Grooming,p-2} \wedge A_{Toileting,p-1} \rightarrow A_{Grooming,p}$
   $cf = 0.58, p_{expected} = 0.001$

5. $A_{Toileting,p-1} \wedge H_{10,p} \nrightarrow A_{Spare\ time/TV,p}$
   $cf = 0.04, p_{unexpected} = 0.03$

World and domain knowledge association rule:

6. $A_{i,p} \xleftrightarrow{Same\ category} A_{j,q} \iff category(i) = category(j)$

Figure 2: Association rule examples. A and H are categorical variables and stand respectively for activity and hour of the day (hours 0-23, not considering minutes). A_i, p stands for a particular type of activity i at position p in the event sequence. cf stands for confidence. $p_{expected}$ and $p_{unexpected}$ are p-values that measure the significance of expected and unexpected association rules, respectively (lower is better).

World and Domain Knowledge Rules: World and domain knowledge can be formalized as rules (C and D in Figure 1). Those rules can be manually entered or come from an existing ontology, for example. The associations they create have the advantage of linking events regardless of their place in the sequence. That means that we can use them to create long-distance links in the text while keeping temporally close events also close in the text.

Rule 6 of Figure 2 is a simple but effective example of a manually entered association rule. It defines a *Same category* association. For the purpose of the ADL example, we arbitrarily grouped the ADL types into categories in the following manner. *Toileting*, *Grooming*, and *Showering* were placed in the category of personal hygiene activities. *Breakfast*, *Lunch*, *Dinner*, and *Snack* were grouped as eating activities. *Spare_Time/TV*, *Leaving*, and *Sleeping* were kept in separate categories.

2.2 Data Interpretation

Step 2 of Figure 1 consists of searching the data to summarize for instances where an association rule applies. Sequential associations are derived from rules such as Rules 2 to 5 from Figure 2. They are shown as arrows going from one row to another at the left of Figure 3. The arrow labels indicate the confidence of the corresponding association rule. Temporal associations are derived from rules such as Rules 1 and 5 from Figure 2. They are indicated by the *Time prob.* and *Temporal association* columns in Figure 3. *Usual* means that an expected association was found and *Unusual* indicates an unexpected association. No indication means that time was not considered significantly useful in predicting those occurrences (no association rule). The probability conditional on time (the confidence of the corresponding association rule candidate) is in any case indicated as it will be used for content selection.

From there, some extra associations are derived and added to the network. The *Repetition* association is generated whenever the type of activity that appears on the right side of the association rule also appears on the left side. *Conjunction* is added when two sequential associations start or end at the same activity. Their other ends are then linked by a *Conjunction* association. The *Instead* association appears when an unexpected association is found. It indicates what would have been the most probable alternate activity according to the sequential association rule model. Derived associations are shown on the right of the first column of Figure 3.

2.3 Event Selection

As can be seen on Figure 1, event selection (step 3) takes as input the associative network and outputs a sub-network of its input. Note that final association selection takes place later, during document structuring, as they are used to build the document structure.

In Figure 3, the output of event selection is shown in bold type. Event selection has one parameter: a maximum probability threshold. Events that have either a probability conditioned on time or an association with a confidence lower or equal to the threshold are selected. In this example, the maximum probability threshold was set to 0.3. Generally the ideal value of the threshold varies in function of

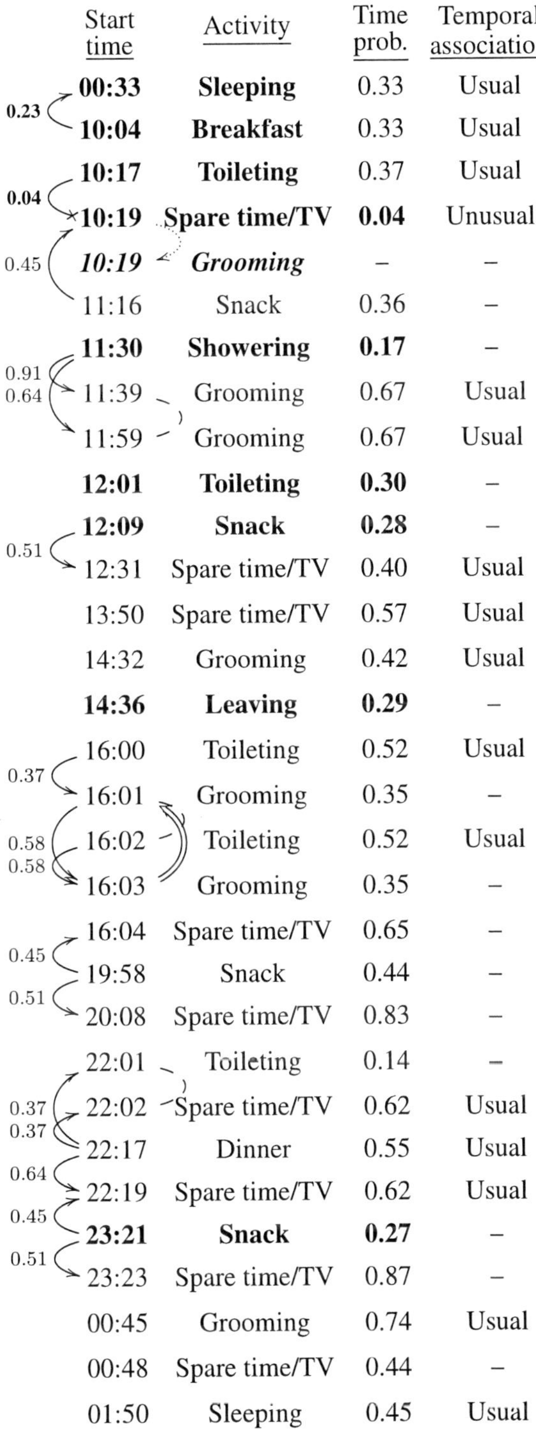

Start time	Activity	Time prob.	Temporal association
00:33	**Sleeping**	0.33	Usual
10:04	**Breakfast**	0.33	Usual
10:17	**Toileting**	0.37	Usual
10:19	**Spare time/TV**	**0.04**	Unusual
10:19	*Grooming*	–	–
11:16	Snack	0.36	–
11:30	**Showering**	0.17	–
11:39	Grooming	0.67	Usual
11:59	Grooming	0.67	Usual
12:01	**Toileting**	**0.30**	–
12:09	**Snack**	**0.28**	–
12:31	Spare time/TV	0.40	Usual
13:50	Spare time/TV	0.57	Usual
14:32	Grooming	0.42	Usual
14:36	**Leaving**	**0.29**	–
16:00	Toileting	0.52	Usual
16:01	Grooming	0.35	–
16:02	Toileting	0.52	Usual
16:03	Grooming	0.35	–
16:04	Spare time/TV	0.65	–
19:58	Snack	0.44	–
20:08	Spare time/TV	0.83	–
22:01	Toileting	0.14	–
22:02	Spare time/TV	0.62	Usual
22:17	Dinner	0.55	Usual
22:19	Spare time/TV	0.62	Usual
23:21	**Snack**	**0.27**	–
23:23	Spare time/TV	0.87	–
00:45	Grooming	0.74	Usual
00:48	Spare time/TV	0.44	–
01:50	Sleeping	0.45	Usual

Figure 3: Associative network for user B on November 24, 2012. The events selected with maximum probability 0.3 are shown in bold type. Sequential associations are on the left. The X-headed arrow represents an unexpected association. On the right are *Instead* (dotted), *Conjunction* (dashed), and *Repetition* (double). *Same category* associations are not shown.

how well the sequential rule model captures what usually happens and the desired average length of the generated text.

2.4 Document Structuring

Connecting Associative Thread: The main goal of document structuring (step 4 in Figure 1) is to give the text a simple narrative structure including a beginning, a middle section, and an end. The importance of this structure for narrative generation was highlighted by a comparison with human written texts (McKinlay et al., 2009). The first event of the period (chronologically) is selected to be the beginning of the text and is called the initial situation (*Sleeping 00:33* in the example of Figure 3). The last event of the period is correspondingly called the final situation (*Sleeping 01:50* in the example). The (rest of the) selected associative sub-network will form the middle section (in bold type in Figure 3). The best event pairs are then chosen to link the selected events with each other. In the example, event pairs with sequential associations are preferred over those with only *Same category* associations. Manually set parameters, called association preferences, define which association types are preferred. They take a value between 0.0 and 1.0. A smaller value gives an event pair with this association type more chances to be chosen. When no other association is present, the default association of temporal proximity is used with association preference 1.0. The association preference is combined (by averaging) with the relative temporal distance in order to favor temporally close event pairs. The resulting score is then used as a distance to compute a minimum spanning tree on the selected associative sub-network.

This minimum spanning tree is converted into a directed rooted tree by designating the initial situation as its root. This tree is hereafter called the connecting associative thread. The path from the initial situation to the final situation is the main associative thread. The other branches of the spanning tree are said to be dead-end threads because once the text has reached their end, it must go back to the connection point with the main thread before continuing toward the final situation. The connecting associative thread connects every event together through the main thread and the dead-end threads. This is illustrated in Figure 4.

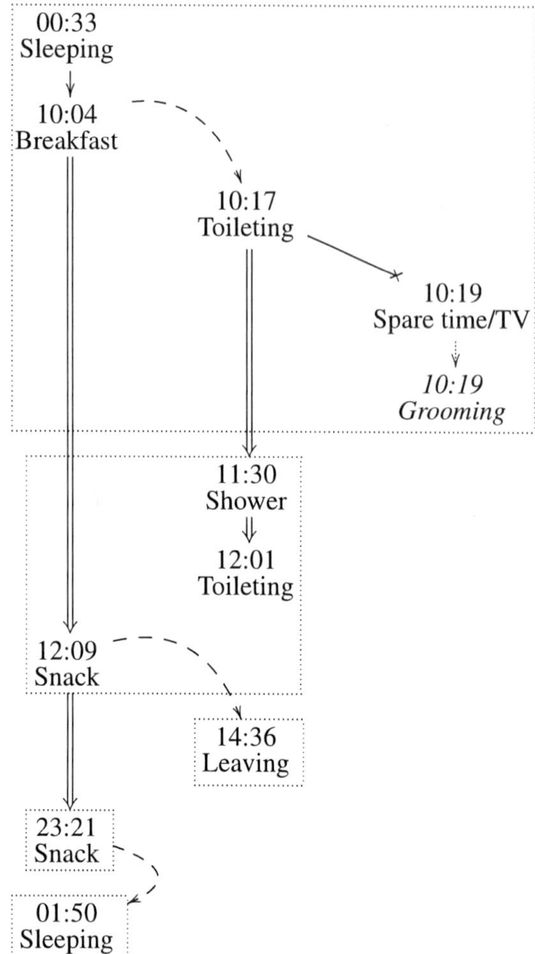

Figure 4: Connecting associative thread for user B on November 24, 2012. Arrows represent associations: simple: expected sequence; X-headed: unexpected sequence; double: *Same category*; dotted: *Instead*; curved and dashed: temporal proximity. Paragraphs are boxed. The vertical order of presentation is the order of mention in the generated text (Figure 5). For event selection, the maximum probability threshold was set to 0.3.

Research on causality in narrative comprehension has uncovered that events on the causal chain going from the beginning to the end of the story are more often recalled than those on dead-end parts of the causal network (Trabasso and van Den Broek, 1985). In the future, it may be interesting to verify if eventualities on the associative sub-threads are less remembered than those on the main associative thread. If this is the case, the content structuring algorithm should be modified to optimize the importance of the expressed associations together with the proportion and importance of the eventualities included in the main associative thread. However taking into account the relative temporal distance in the computation of the minimum spanning tree already tends to avoid a too short main associative thread.

Paragraph and Sentence Segmentation: The document content is then segmented into sentences and paragraphs. The style can be varied by adjusting two parameters: the average number of events introduced in one sentence and the average number of sentences in one paragraph. Those parameters are used to calculate the number of breaks needed between sentences and paragraphs. The candidate break points are between consecutive event pairs in the document plan. The actual break points are selected according to the distance computed previously for the determination of the minimum spanning tree. The greatest distances correspond to paragraph breaks, then sentence breaks, and lastly phrase boundaries. Paragraphs are boxed in Figure 4.

At this point, a mapping is made between the selected associations and the rhetorical relations that will be expressed in the text. In the example, sequential associations are expressed by a Temporal Sequence relation and *Same category* associations are expressed by a Conjunction relation.

2.5 Microplanning

Microplanning (step 5 of Figure 1) translates the rhetorical structure into a lexico-syntactic specification. Each sentence plan tree is traversed depth-first. When a leaf is visited, a specification of the corresponding eventuality's description is produced from lexico-syntactic templates. When an internal node is visited, the rhetorical relations linking the two children nodes are expressed with appropriate discourse markers. Those markers are then used to assemble the lexico-syntactic specifications obtained from the children nodes.

However the marking of rhetorical relations between sentences is handled differently. Each sentence has a main event, which is the one expressed by its first independent clause. The main event of a paragraph is the main event of its first sentence. A rhetorical relation marker is placed at the front of a sentence to indicate its parent relation in the connecting associative thread. If its parent is the main event of the preceding sentence, or main event of the preceding paragraph in the case of the first sentence of a paragraph, the marker appears alone. If not, an anaphoric expression is added that restates the parent event. For example, the parent of *Toileting 12:01* in Figure 4 is *Shower 11:40*. Since it is the main event of the preceding sentence, no anaphor is added and we have just the marker *also* in the generated text (Figure 5). On the contrary, the parent of *Snack 12:09* is *Breakfast 10:04*. It is located in another paragraph. Consequently, the marker becomes *beside his 10:04 PM breakfast*.

2.6 Surface Realization

Surface realization (step 6 of Figure 1) was performed using the SimpleNLG-EnFr Java library (Vaudry and Lapalme, 2013). During surface realization, the syntactic and lexical specifications are combined with the output language grammar and lexicon to generate formatted natural language text. The lexico-syntactic templates used in microplanning were written for both English and French output languages. In combination with SimpleNLG-EnFr, this enabled bilingual generation.

An example of English generated text corresponding to the preceding figures is given in Figure 5.

2.7 Human Reading

Finally, in step 7 of Figure 1 a human reader combines his world and domain knowledge with the generated text to construct a causal mental representation of the events. For that the reader can follow the connecting associative thread through the text while trying to infer possible causal relations.

We hypothesize that statistically identifying sequential associations is a useful pre-processing of the data for the purpose of determining causal relations. Association rules based on type could also be helpful because events of the same type sometimes have the same cause or the same type of cause. Other association rules based on such causal reasoning could also give useful hints. In any case, the reader can choose to ignore irrelevant associations.

For example, the fact that the clauses expressing *Sleeping 00:33* and *Breakfast 10:04* are coordinated in the same sentence and linked by the temporal marker *then* could lead the reader to different conclusions depending of his knowledge. On one hand, he could think that maybe the user was particularly

```
OrdonezB Saturday, 24 November
2012 12:33 AM - Sunday,
25 November 2012 09:24 AM
------------------------------------

OrdonezB got up at 10:02 AM and then
he ate his breakfast.  As usual at
10:17 AM he went to the toilet but
then he unexpectedly spent 1 hour in
the living room instead of grooming.

In addition to having gone to the
toilet at 10:17 AM, he took a shower
at 11:30 AM. Also at 12:01 PM he went
to the toilet.  Beside his 10:04 AM
breakfast, he had a snack at 12:09
PM.

At 2:36 PM he left for 1 hour.

In addition to his 12:09 PM snack, he
had a snack at 11:21 PM.

As usual at 1:50 AM he went to bed.
```

Figure 5: Generated text example for user B on November 24, 2012. The maximum probability threshold was set to 0.3.

hungry when he woke up that morning; he could ponder why. On the other hand, he could also ignore this sequence as just a random happening. Another example: the fact that *Snack 23:21* references *Snack 12:09* could make the reader conclude that maybe the user was often hungry on that day and maybe there was a common cause for that. Or the reader may ignore this, reasoning that *Snack 12:09* was probably in reality a *Lunch* activity. The point is that some of the associations can help the reader in forming causal hypotheses. The reader can later verify those, for example by asking the user. Moreover, those causal hypotheses can help the reader remember the content of the text.

3 Evaluation

We asked judges to evaluate the textual quality of the reports. To assemble the evaluation corpus, a report was generated for the 32 complete days (starting and ending with a long *Sleeping* activity) of the dataset. The selection parameter was adjusted in order that texts for both users have comparable average length. The maximum probability threshold was thus set to

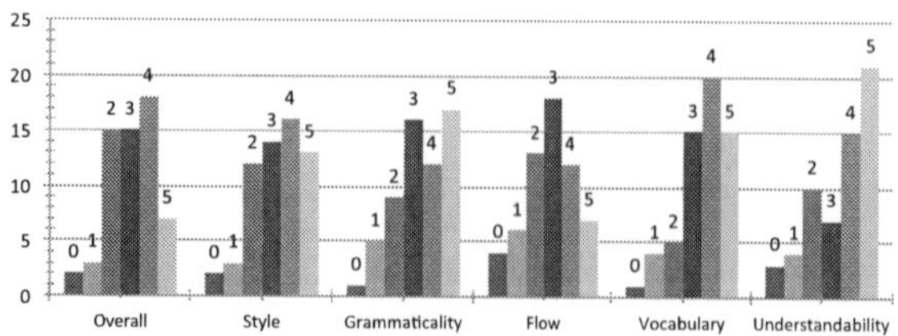

Figure 6: Results of the text quality evaluation.

0.4 for user A and 0.3 for user B. User A's routine seems to be easier to capture by the sequential rule model than user B's. Hence the probability for user A's activities is generally higher than for user B's.

Because no human-written equivalent of the generated ADL reports exists, it would have been meaningless to try to write some to make the comparison. Therefore only the generated texts are evaluated.

13 judges evaluated four to five generated texts each, so that 28 texts were evaluated by two judges each and 4 texts by one judge. The judges had to evaluate the texts on a 0 to 5 scale for six criteria: Overall, Style, Grammaticality, Flow (between sentences), Vocabulary, and Understandability. They could also leave comments. The evaluation forms, generated texts and answers are publicly available[1].

If we view all the evaluations taken together as evaluating the data-to-text system as a whole, as opposed to individual texts, we get the results shown in Figure 6. The best ratings are for Understandability and Vocabulary with peaks at 5 and 4, respectively. The worst ratings are for Flow with a peak at 3. This could indicate some deficiencies in document planning and/or microplanning. However, according to the good Understandability ratings, the texts do not seem as badly planned as to be confusing. The results for Grammaticality are hard to interpret, since there are two peaks: one at 3 and one at 5. By looking at the evaluations, we think it could be because this criterion was not defined clearly enough. Overall and Style have most ratings ranging from 2 to 5, with peaks at 4.

4   Related Work

Chambers and Jurafsky (2008) learn narrative event chains (partially ordered sets of events with a common protagonist) from a news stories corpus. For

this they use pointwise mutual information (PMI) to measure the relation between two events, instead of the probability of independence according to the binomial distribution. They then use a temporal classifier to determine a partial order. Finally, they cluster events using the PMI scores to form in effect undirected n-ary associations. Those could be converted to directed associations if confidence was also computed.

With the help of focus and inferencing models, Niehaus and Young (2014) generate narratives in which some events need to be causally inferred by the reader. Those inferences are precisely defined as part of the input, whereas in our model only hints are available about the causal relations to be found by the reader.

León and Gervás (2010) also use causality-related relations to structure narratives. Their algorithm learns preconditional rules between events of a fictional story with the help of human feedback. An assumption is made that every event must be directly or indirectly a precondition to the last event of the story. Although this may make sense for a fictional story, it could involve selecting out important information when starting from real-life data.

In the context of generating a narrative from data with multiple actors, Gervás (2014) associates actions having the same actor. This makes sense, because actions by the same actor can certainly be directly or indirectly causally related. However, our prototype having been tested only on data with a single actor, this tactic would not have been adequate here.

Farrell et al. (2015) use regular expressions to define explanation specifications for error trace data. Regular expressions could also be used to manually define association rules in the context of our model.

Baez Miranda et al. (2014) use a task model to provide top-down constraints on the sequence of scenes that can be identified in the data to form the structure of the narrative. In contrast, our model can be said to be more bottom-up in the importance it gives to automatically extracted associations.

In Vaudry and Lapalme (2015), we tried to structure the narrative using hierarchical clustering. This did not achieve a structure fully labeled with rhetorical relations as our current spanning tree algorithm. Paragraph and sentence segmentation was less transparent since we did not use dedicated parameters. Furthermore we extracted only chronological sequential association rules. We interpreted this chronological direction as the direction of causality. This partly justified our claim of identifying approximate causal relations. By looking at the results of data interpretation, we now come to the conclusion that there is no clear link between the direction of the rule and the direction of a potential causal relation.

In addition, we selected which events to include in the text in what we called the summarization step, which we placed after document planning. This has the disadvantage of undoing some of the document planner's work. We selected events using the probability of this event type happening at any point in the event sequence. We now find that using the probability conditioned on time results in a greater proportion of the associative sub-network being connected. This leads to a better text structure. Note that we use for our current example the same data as before, with a maximum probability threshold of 0.3 instead of 0.4.

5 Conclusion

We presented a data-to-text model demonstrating that it is possible to structure a narrative around a mix of automatically mined and manually defined associations. The model also relies on sequential associations for event selection. The generated text's communicative goal is to help the reader assimilate the facts necessary to construct a causal representation of the events. According to the model, the connecting associative thread allows the reader to follow associations from the beginning to the end of the text. This structure takes the form of a spanning tree over a selected associative sub-network.

The textual quality of the generated texts was rated by judges. The results show that the texts were understandable, but that flow between sentences, although not bad, could still be improved. A possible solution would be to modify document structuring such as to minimize discontinuities. According to the event-indexing model (Zwaan et al., 1995), sentence-reading times increase with the number of discontinuities in temporality, spatiality, protagonist, causality, or intentionality.

We are currently designing a memorization experiment to test if the generated texts help the reader assimilate unusual facts independently of the domain. Apart from that, a task-oriented evaluation with domain experts could be organized. Furthermore texts could be generated from bigger datasets or datasets belonging to other domains. It would be interesting to fine-tune all parameters for each of those to see if ideal values vary from domain to domain.

References

Belén A Baez Miranda, Sybille Caffiau, Catherine Garbay, and François Portet. 2014. Task based model for récit generation from sensor data: an early experiment. In *5th International Workshop on Computational Models of Narrative*, pages 1–10.

Mieke Bal. 2009. *Narratology : introduction to the theory of narrative*. University of Toronto Press, Toronto, 3rd ed. edition.

Nadjet Bouayad-Agha, Gerard Casamayor, Simon Mille, and Leo Wanner. 2012. Perspective-oriented Generation of Football Match Summaries: Old Tasks, New Challenges. *ACM Trans. Speech Lang. Process.*, 9(2):3:1–3:31, August.

Nathanael Chambers and Daniel Jurafsky. 2008. Unsupervised Learning of Narrative Event Chains. In *ACL*, volume 94305, pages 789–797. Citeseer.

Rachel Farrell, Gordon Pace, and M Rosner. 2015. A Framework for the Generation of Computer System Diagnostics in Natural Language using Finite State Methods. In *Proceedings of the 15th European Workshop on Natural Language Generation (ENLG)*, pages 52–56, Brighton, UK, September. Association for Computational Linguistics.

Pablo Gervás. 2014. Composing narrative discourse for stories of many characters: A case study over a chess game. *Literary and Linguistic Computing*, August.

Catalina Hallett. 2008. Multi-modal presentation of medical histories. In *Proceedings of the 13th international conference on Intelligent user interfaces*, pages 80–89.

James Hunter, Yvonne Freer, Albert Gatt, Ehud Reiter, Somayajulu Sripada, and Cindy Sykes. 2012. Automatic generation of natural language nursing shift summaries in neonatal intensive care: BT-Nurse. *Artificial intelligence in medicine*.

Anna Jordanous. 2012. A standardised procedure for evaluating creative systems: Computational creativity evaluation based on what it is to be creative. *Cognitive Computation*, 4(3):246–279.

Carlos León and Pablo Gervás. 2010. Towards a Black Box Approximation to Human Processing of Narratives Based on Heuristics over Surface Form. In *2010 AAAI Fall Symposium Series*, November.

William C. Mann and Sandra A. Thompson. 1987. *Rhetorical structure theory: A theory of text organization*. University of Southern California, Information Sciences Institute.

A. McKinlay, C. McVittie, E. Reiter, Y. Freer, C. Sykes, and R. Logie. 2009. Design Issues for Socially Intelligent User Interfaces: A Discourse Analysis of a Data-to-text System for Summarizing Clinical Data. *Methods of Information in Medicine*, 49(4):379–387, December.

James Niehaus and R. Michael Young. 2014. Cognitive models of discourse comprehension for narrative generation. *Literary and Linguistic Computing*, 29(4):561–582, December.

Fco Javier Ordóñez, Paula de Toledo, and Araceli Sanchis. 2013. Activity Recognition Using Hybrid Generative/Discriminative Models on Home Environments Using Binary Sensors. *Sensors*, 13(5):5460–5477, April.

Ivo Swartjes and Marit Theune. 2006. A fabula model for emergent narrative. In *Technologies for Interactive Digital Storytelling and Entertainment*, pages 49–60. Springer.

Marit Theune, Nanda Slabbers, and Feikje Hielkema. 2007. The Narrator: NLG for digital storytelling. In *Proceedings of the Eleventh European Workshop on Natural Language Generation*, pages 109–112. Association for Computational Linguistics.

Tom Trabasso and Paul van Den Broek. 1985. Causal Thinking and the Representation of Narrative Events. *Journal of Memory and Language*, 24(5):612–630, October.

Tom Trabasso, Paul Van den Broek, and So Young Suh. 1989. Logical necessity and transitivity of causal relations in stories. *Discourse Processes*, 12(1):1–25.

Pierre-Luc Vaudry and Guy Lapalme. 2013. Adapting SimpleNLG for bilingual English-French realisation. In *Proceedings of the 14th European Workshop on Natural Language Generation*, pages 183–187, Sofia, Bulgaria, August. Association for Computational Linguistics.

Pierre-Luc Vaudry and Guy Lapalme. 2015. Narrative Generation from Extracted Associations. In *Proceedings of the 15th European Workshop on Natural Language Generation*, pages 136–145, Brighton, United Kingdom, September. Association for Computational Linguistics.

Leo Wanner, Bernd Bohnet, Nadjet Bouayad-Agha, Franois Lareau, and Daniel Nickla. 2010. Marquis: Generation of User-Tailored Multilingual Air Quality Bulletins. *Applied Artificial Intelligence*, 24(10):914–952.

Rolf A. Zwaan, Mark C. Langston, and Arthur C. Graesser. 1995. The Construction of Situation Models in Narrative Comprehension: An Event-Indexing Model. *Psychological Science*, 6(5):292–297, September.

Human-like Natural Language Generation Using Monte Carlo Tree Search

Kaori Kumagai   Ichiro Kobayashi
Ochanomizu University
{kaori.kumagai,koba}@is.ocha.ac.jp

Daichi Mochihashi
The Institute of Statistical Mathematics
daichi@ism.ac.jp

Hideki Asoh
AIST
h.asoh@aist.go.jp

Tomoaki Nakamura   Takayuki Nagai
University of Electro-Communications
{tnakamura,tnagai}@ee.uec.ac.jp

Abstract

We propose a method of probabilistic natural language generation observing both a syntactic structure and an input of situational content. We employed Monte Carlo Tree Search for this nontrivial search problem, employing context-free grammar rules as search operators and evaluating numerous putative generations from these two aspects using logistic regression and n-gram language model. Through several experiments, we confirmed that our method can effectively generate sentences with various words and phrasings.

1   Introduction

People unconsciously produce utterances in daily life according to different situations. When a person encounters a situation in which a dog eats a piece of bread, he or she retrieves appropriate words and creates a natural sentence, retaining the dependent relationships among the words in proper order, to describe the situation. This ability of natural language generation (NLG) from situations will become essential for robotics and conversational agents in the future.

However, this problem is intrinsically difficult because it is hard to encode what to say into a sentence while ensuring its syntactic correctness. We propose to use Monte Carlo tree search (MCTS) (Kocsis and Szepesvari, 2006; Browne et al., 2012), a stochastic search algorithm for decision processes, to find an optimal solution in the decision space. We build a search tree of possible syntactic trees to generate a sentence, by selecting proper rules through numerous random simulations of possible yields.

2   NLG with MCTS simulations

2.1   MCTS

MCTS combines random simulation and best-first search in its search process (Kocsis and Szepesvari, 2006). It has been successfully applied as an algorithm for playing Go game and similar planning problems. In fact, both Go game and NLG share the same characteristic: their outputs can be evaluated only when their process reaches the last state. Therefore, we think that the process of NLG can be represented in MCTS simulations.

MCTS uses the upper confidence bounds one (UCB1) value to determine the next move from a viewpoint of multi-armed bandit problem (Katehakis and Veinott, 1987):

$$\text{UCB1} = v_i + C\sqrt{\frac{\log N}{n_i}}. \tag{1}$$

Here, v_i is the winning rate of candidate i, C is an adjustment coefficient, N is the total number of simulations, and n_i is the number of visits to the candidate i. The first term of equation (1) corresponds to exploitation and the second term corresponds to exploration in simulation, achieving a balanced search between the two factors (Auer et al., 2002).

2.2   Algorithm

MCTS provides opportunities for selecting various syntactic structures and words in a generated sentence in our case. We use context-free grammar (CFG) rules obtained from the *Brown corpus* as a search operator in MCTS. The MCTS algorithm is shown in Figure 1

11

Proceedings of the INLG 2016 Workshop on Computational Creativity and Natural Language Generation, pages 11–18,
Edinburgh, September 2016. ©2016 Association for Computational Linguistics

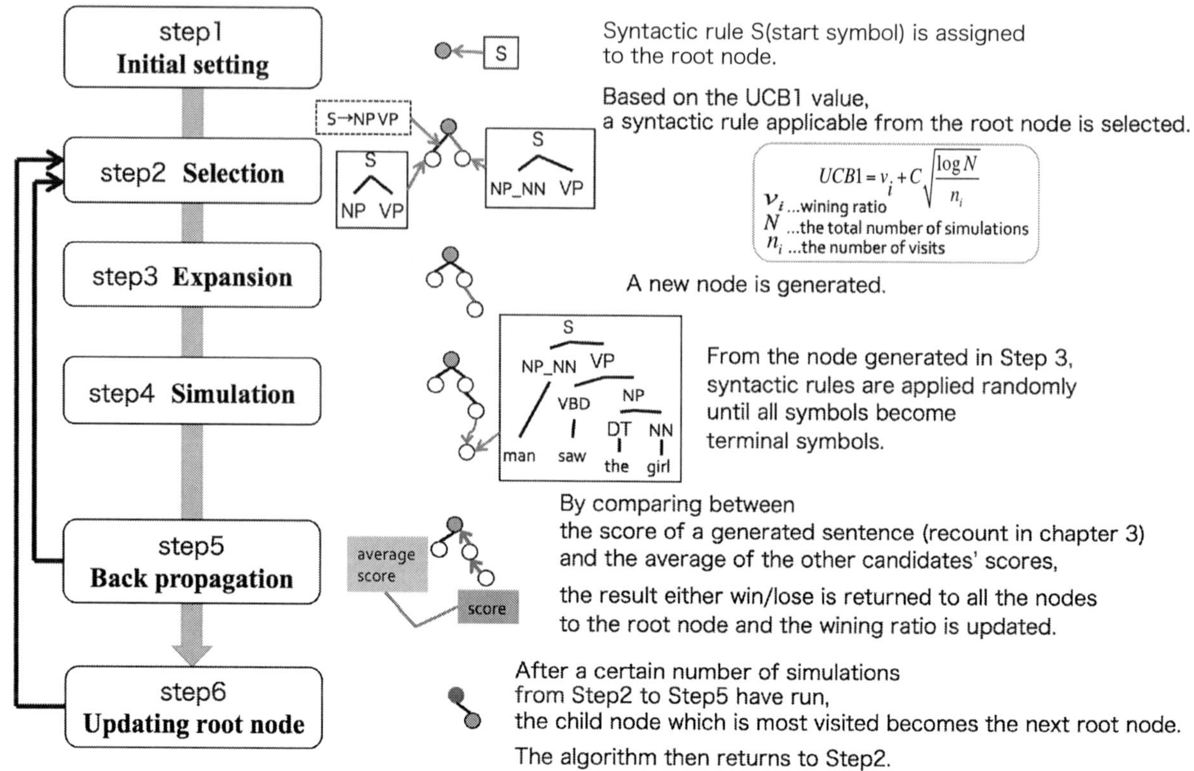

Figure 1: MCTS algorithm for NLG

Essentially, our MCTS builds a search space of possible derivations, and starting from the initial symbol S we iteratively determine what rule to apply to extend the current tree, by simulating numerous possible derivations from the candidate rules.

3   Evaluating generated sentences

When using MCTS in NLG, it is important how the simulation result, i.e., a generated sentence, is evaluated. In generating a sentence, unlike playing Go game, it is not easy for a machine to decide whether a generated sentence is natural for us because the result cannot be naturally represented by a win or a lose. This necessitates giving machines the ability to evaluate whether a generated sentence is natural or not. Regarding this problem, Okanohara and Tsujii (2007) proposed a method to use a semi-Markov class model to identify the grammaticality of the sentence. Similarly, in this study we have introduced two evaluation scores: one for syntactic structure and the other for the n-gram language model.

3.1   Evaluation of syntactic structure

For this purpose, we use logistic regression with partial syntactic trees of a sentence as its features for identifying whether it is natural or not. Figure 2 illustrates the procedure of building a classifier for structure evaluation.

We used the *Brown corpus*[1] and extracted 4,661 sentences consisting of three to seven words other than punctuation marks. Those extracted sentences were parsed using the *Stanford parser*[2], and a set of *CFGs* was created based on its result. The *CFGs* contained 7,220 grammar rules and 5,867 terminal symbols.

As the training data for the classifier, we regard syntactic subtrees of sentences in the *Brown corpus* as the positive examples, and subtrees of the sentences generated from random simulation of *CFGs* as negative examples.

As we see in Figure 2, we have prepared 46,610

---

[1] http://clu.uni.no/icame/browneks.html
[2] http://nlp.stanford.edu/software/lex-parser.shtml

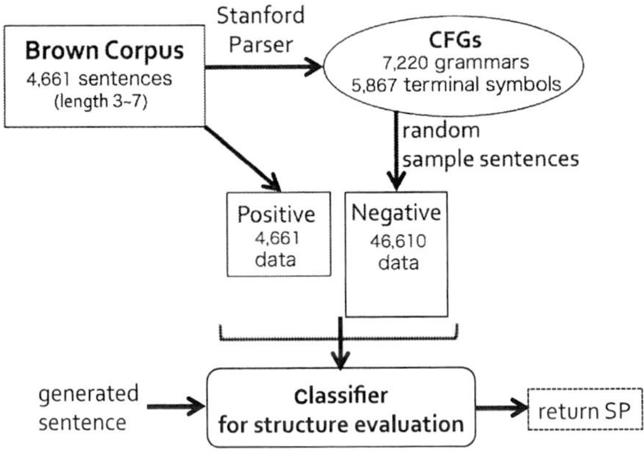

Figure 2: Building a classifier for structured sentences.

syntactically incorrect sentences as negative examples – the reason why there are ten times as many negative examples as positive examples is that it is highly possible that more syntactically incorrect than correct sentences can be generated using MCTS simulations with *CFGs*.

We use FREQuent Tree miner (FREQT)[3] to extract syntactic subtrees of sentences (Abe et al., 2002; Zaki, 2002). From all of the subtrees obtained, we use the subtrees from which only the terminal symbols have been removed as the features for the classifier, because of our exclusive focus on syntactic structure with nonterminal symbols. We call the probability of the output from this classifier as Syntactic Probability (SP) (see, Figure 2).

We evaluated the classifier with 10-fold cross validation and obtained 98% accuracy for the test data.

3.2 Evaluation for n-gram language model

To evaluate the word sequence in a generated sentence, we conducted an experiment to compare the accuracy of evaluation between two kinds of the n-gram based scores. One is the score calculating the perplexity of trigrams with Kneser-Ney smoothing. We call this score 'PP'. The other is the score called Acceptability proposed in Lau et al. (2015), which measures the acceptability of a sentence for an English native speaker. In this study, we use the Acceptability (AP) below for a sentence s:

$$Acceptability(s) = \log \left(\frac{p(s)}{p_{\text{uni}}(s)} \right)^{\frac{1}{|s|}} \quad (2)$$

---
[3]http://chasen.org/˜taku/software/freqt/

As an n-gram language model $p(s)$, we use trigrams with Kneser-Ney smoothing (Kneser and Ney, 1995). In (2), $p_{\text{uni}}(s)$ denotes the probability with a unigram distribution and (2) measures a relative fluency per word as compared to baseline probability p_{uni}.

3.3 How to decide the win/lose of sentences

At the Step 5 in the MCTS algorithm, the final decision of a win or a lose (1 or 0) about the sentence is returned by the score based on the 'SP' and 'PP or AP' decisions as follows: (i) if it wins on both 'SP' and 'PP or AP', the score is 1; (ii) if it fails with 'SP', the score is 0; (iii) if it wins on 'SP' but fails on 'PP or AP', the score is 0.5. This reflects our assumption that the generated sentence from *CFGs* must be syntactical at least. Those processes of (i), (ii), and (iii) are summarized in Table 1.

Table 1: How to determine the final decision

SP	PP or AP	score
0	0	0
0	1	0
1	0	0.5
1	1	1

4 Generation with Situational Information

We have so far discussed *"how to say"* part of NLG. Next, we consider *"what to say"* in terms of how to flexibly choose words that are suitable for a given situation. We will explain how words are chosen in a generated sentence with the linguistic resources shown in Figure 3.

Let us assume that some words have been specified as the content to speak about, say "dog" and "run" (*Given words* in Figure 3) and we consider how to incorporate them into the sentence to generate. There are multiple ways to describe the content with natural language sentences. For example, we could say "dog" as "puppy" or "run" as "dash". Therefore, considering the possibility of flexibly choosing words, we used *word2vec* (Mikolov et al., 2013) trained on Wikipedia to determine the set of similar words whose cosine distance > 0.5 as the dictionary (*Similar words*). Further, in order to adding the peripheral words of the given words to

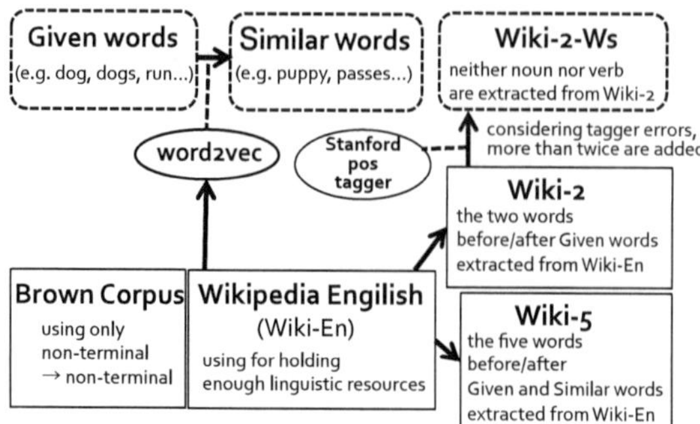

Figure 3: Relationship between linguistic resources. Boxes with dashed lines are used as dictionaries for generation within MCTS.

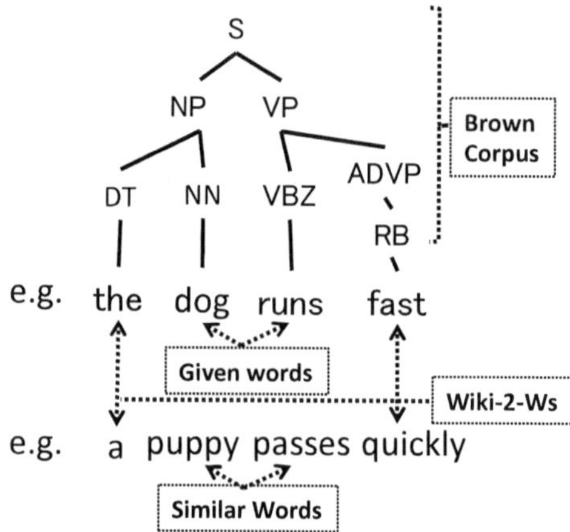

Figure 4: Example of a generated sentence.

the dictionary, we prepared another dictionary from two words window before/after of the given words on Wikipedia as the candidate words other than noun or verbs (*Wiki-2-Ws*). During generation, we generate sentences using these dictionaries depending on the part-of-speech of each word to reduce the search space, and classified a sentence as "lose" when it contains words out of the *Given words* and *Similar words*. *Wiki-5* is the statistics from five-words window before/after of the *Given words* and the *Similar words* on Wikipedia to compute AP or PP.

Figure 4 illustrates a generated syntax tree example with the linguistic resources shown in Figure 3.

Note that selecting proper linguistic resources is a nontrivial problem for generation: because there are huge number of possibilities to use them with different syntactic trees, it requires a ingenious method like MCTS to effectively combine them with a grammatical tree as well as retaining fluency with respect to n-gram probabilities. We used the information to feed as a bag of words for simplicity, and aim to use more sophisticated use of input as a distinct problem from the proposed algorithm.

5 Related studies

As for the nondeterministic approach to NLG, some studies view NLG as a planning problem. Koller and Stone (2007) used automated classical planning techniques to derive a plan converted into a sentence. Kondadadi et al. (2013) consolidated macro and micro planning as well as surface realization stages into one statistical learning process. As another way to handle the indeterminate characteris-

tics of NLG, Lemon (2008; 2011) and Rieser and Lemon (2009) modeled dialog as Markov decision processes (MDPs) and solved them by means of reinforcement learning (Sutton and Barto, 1998).

Similar to our approach, McKinley and Ray (2014) considered the NLG process as an MDP with a suitably defined reward function to achieve efficient sentence generation using an MCTS algorithm. As another nondeterministic approach using a neural language model (Bengio et al., 2003), Wen et al. (2015) used the Long Short-term Memory generator, which can learn from unaligned data by concurrently optimizing sentence planning and surface realization using a simple cross-entropy training criterion and easily achieve language variation by sampling from output candidates. However, this method predicts just a word sequence and does not consider syntactic structures.

As another search-based algorithm to generate a sentence considering syntactic structures, Liu et al. (2015) proposed a syntactic linearization of given words using beam-search for an appropriate structure of a sentence. However, it just treats the problem of word ordering and does not consider generations with the given words, which does not always include the given words in themselves. Technically, their method employs a beam search with a predefined beamwidth. On the other hand, MCTS realizes an efficient search that does not restrict the search range in advance.

Moreover, Silver et al. (2016) developed AlphaGo which defeated a top level professional Go player.

They combined MCTS with a deep reinforcement learning framework and then provided MCTS with learning ability; both policy and value networks of the system are trained to predict human expert behaviors using deep reinforcement learning. This framework is expected to be applied to NLG in the future.

6 Experiments

In this section, we conducted experiments with two cases where we evaluate only syntactic structure of a generated sentence, and evaluate both syntactic structure and n-gram language model characteristic of a generated sentence.

6.1 Experimental settings

We used the *CFGs* and the classifier to evaluate the structure of a sentence mentioned in section 3.1.

In addition, we set the number of MCTS simulations at a node as the number of wins that reach five times as many as other candidate nodes at that time. The reason we used a dynamic change of simulation number is that the next root node must be chosen based on a clear difference in winning percentage compared to other candidate nodes.

6.2 Evaluation for syntactic structure

First, we focus on only syntactic structure, and conducted generation experiments to evaluate it. As the evaluation score for a generated sentence, we employ only 'SP'. Table 3 shows some generated sentences.

Looking at the above sentences, we see that they are syntactically correct – they have syntactic structure of either SVO or SV. The scores of them are approximately 0.99, therefore, we see that correct

Table 3: Generated sentences based on the evaluation for only syntactic structure

Generated sentences	SP
all mass nudged no teacher	0.999
this principle observed all super-condamine	0.999
all kay sank all round	0.999
some camping departs	0.994
those rim made these amount	0.999

syntactic structure are apparently generated based on the classifier.

6.3 Generation with two evaluation indices

Next, we conducted an experiment based on both evaluation criteria for syntactic structure and an n-gram language model. The 'win' or 'lose' is decided as explained in section 3.3.

Furthermore, in order to confirm that we can generate sentences of various lengths, we introduce a constraint on sentence length: if a generated sentence has a length shorter than the predefined length, the simulation result is regarded as a lose. Moreover, as mentioned in section 3.2, we used PP and AP to compare the results evaluated by them.

Here, because lower perplexity is better, the simulation result is regarded as a win when the score is less than the average of those of other candidate nodes. Table 2 shows some generated sentences.

From the results shown in Table 2, we see that syntactically correct sentences are generated. In the case of using AP, we also see that low frequency words were selected in generating sentences, and a sentence is generated without any influence from word frequency. On the other hand, we have confirmed that when a generated sentence is evaluated by PP, the sentence is influenced more by word fre-

Table 2: Generation with AP and PP

Length	Generated sentences	SP	AP
5	those memorial neglected neither contraction-extension	0.999	85.46
6	all marketing half-straightened neither contraction-extension understandingly	0.999	91.79

Length	Generated sentences	SP	PP
5	no theirs defied no improvement	0.999	1008.63
6	no one said his own work	0.999	156.85

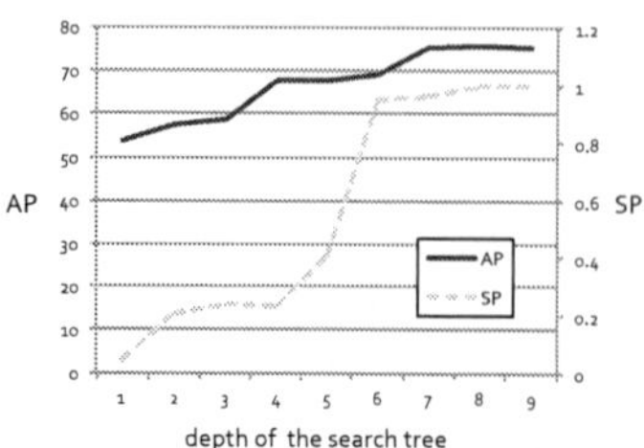

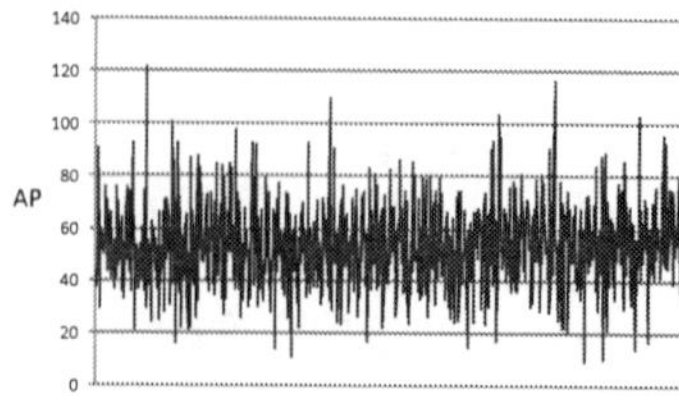
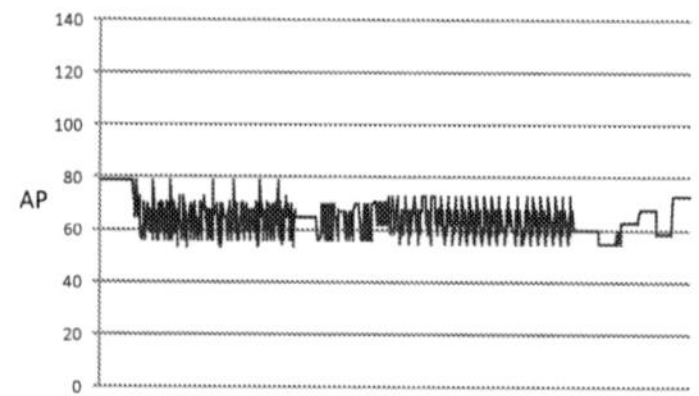

(a) Depths of MCTS search space with respect to acceptability and syntactic correctness.

(b) Acceptability scores: Initial 1,000 simulations.

(c) Acceptability scores: Last 1,000 simulations.

Figure 5: Statistics during MCTS simulations to generate a sentence from the situation {*boy, play, basketball*}.

quency than when AP is used.

7 Experiment with situational information

In this experiment, we aim to generate sentences with specific words as given situational information.

7.1 Experimental settings

We use the same linguistic resources mentioned in section 4. In the experiment, we dealt with three cases where the content for a generated sentence has the words, either "dog, run", "dog, eat, bread", or "boy, play, basketball".

As for lexical selection, we put a constraint that a word to generate must have positive bigram counts from the preceding word in the Wiki-5 statistics. Setting this constraint avoids unlikely words in advance to achieve more appropriate lexical selection within MTCS framework.

Furthermore, as for the constraints on the number of simulations and on the length of a generated sentence, they are the same settings mentioned in section 6.1 and 6.3, respectively.

7.2 Experimental results

Table 4 shows an example of generated sentences from different situations. Comparing AP with PP, when AP is used, a wide variety of words are selected. As a concrete example, in the case where the words "dog", "eat" and "bread" are specified, when PP was used for evaluation of the n-gram language model, the word "every" was selected as an adjective many times. In contrast, when AP was used, words such as "another", "neither" and "all" were selected.

Figure 5(a) shows the trends in the average values of AP and SP whenever the root node is updated

in MCTS simulations with an example of generating a sentence with the specified words {*boy, play, basketball*}. We see that the value of SP is approximately 0.1 initially and then converges around 0.99 as exploration deepens. As for AP, we have not observed any clear convergence in the exploration process, however, at the initial stage of exploration we have observed instead that generated sentences do not satisfy the generation constraints, e.g., whose length is too short or too long, therefore, the values of more than 100 or less than 20 have been observed. Figures 5(b) and 5(c) shows the values of AP of the initial and final 1,000 simulations, respectively. From these figures, we see that AP converges to a particular value.

For the output of situation (a) in Table 4 "*every dog runs her cat*", we have observed the sentences that resulted in "lose" during the generation in Table 5.

Table 5: Sentences that resulted in "lose" to generate *every dog runs her cat* during the MCTS generation.

Sentence	SP	AP
be more in	0.126	28.03
be shall run or dog american	0.056	41.41
either dog was puppy	0.999	46.76
le dog runs his mr. three	0.999	34.14

8 Conclusions

In this paper, we proposed the first attempt to exploit MCTS for natural language generation. Because MCTS allows a stochastic search using the possible yields, namely the sentence from the current point of search, we can leverage both the syntactic structure (CFG) and statistical fluency (n-grams)

Table 4: NLG with situational information. Situation of (a) = {*dog,run*}, (b) = {*dog,eat,bread*}, (c) = {*boy,play,basketball*}.

Situ.	Len	Generated sentences	SP	AP
(a)	4	either dog runs his cat	0.999	39.95
	5	every dog runs her cat	0.999	37.13
(b)	5	every dog eats his bread	0.999	37.58
	5	another dog eats his bread	0.999	42.73
	6	neither dog eats its own bread	0.999	42.71
	6	all dog eats its original bread	0.999	41.33
(c)	5	girls tennis played the rugby	0.998	59.65
	5	volleyball boys played both rugby	0.998	72.03
	6	girls tennis was played senior football	0.996	71.96
	6	girls tennis played played and los	0.996	66.55

Situ.	Len	Generated sentences	SP	PP
(a)	4	this cat is run	0.999	76.87
	5	some dog runs his cat	0.999	350.72
(b)	5	every dog eats his bread	0.999	310.92
	5	no dog eats its flour	0.999	383.59
	6	every dog eats its first flour	0.999	380.06
	6	every dog eats its original bread	0.999	358.97
(c)	5	boys soccer played the tennis	0.999	317.28
	5	girls tennis played an football	0.999	448.10
	6	le boy plays her own tennis	0.999	549.45
	6	boys tennis was played to all the	0.996	114.92

through a logistic regression to determine the "win" or "lose" of generated sentences.

While our results are still preliminary using limited linguistic resources, we believe this method is beneficial for future NLG integrating both the syntax and semantics in an ingenious statistical way.

References

K. Abe, S. Kawasoe, T. Asai, H. Arimura, and S. Arikawa. 2002. Optimized substructure discovery for semi-structured data. In *PKDD 2002*, volume 6, pages 1–14.

P. Auer, N. Cesa-Bianchi, and P. Fischer. 2002. Finite-time analysis of the multi-armed bandit problem. *Machine Learning*, 47:235–256.

Y. Bengio, R. Ducharme, P. Vincent, and C. Janvin. 2003. A neural probabilistic language model. *Journal of Machine Learning Research*, 3:1137–1155.

C. Browne, E. Powley, D. Whitehouse, S. Lucas, P. I. Cowling, P. Rohlfshagen, S. Tavener, D. Perez, S. Samothrakis, and S. Colton. 2012. Survey of monte carlo tree search methods. *IEEE Transactions on Computational Intelligence and AI in Games*, 4(1).

M. N. Katehakis and A. F. Veinott. 1987. The multi-armed bandit problem : Decomposition and computation. *Mathematics of Operations Research*, 12(2):262–268.

R. Kneser and H. Ney. 1995. Improved backing-off for m-gram language modeling. In *ICASSP*, volume 1, pages 181–184.

L. Kocsis and C. Szepesvari. 2006. Bandit based monte carlo planning. In *ECML 2006*, pages 282–293.

A. Koller and M. Stone. 2007. Sentence generation as a planning problem. In *International Natural Language Generation Workshop*, volume 12, pages 17–24.

R. Kondadadi, B. Howald, and F. Schilder. 2013. A statistical nlg framework for aggregated planning and realization. In *ACL 2013*, volume 51, pages 1406–1415.

J. H. Lau, A. Clark, and S. Lappin. 2015. Unsupervised prediction of acceptability judgements. In *ACL 2015*, volume 53, pages 15–1000.

O. Lemon. 2008. Adaptive natural language generation in dialogue using reinforcement learning. In *Workshop on the Semantics and Pragmatics of Dialogue (SEM-DIAL)*, pages 141–148.

O. Lemon. 2011. Learning what to say and how to say it:joint optimization of spoken dialogue management and natural language generation. *Computer Speech and Language*, 25(2):210–221.

Y. Liu, Y. Zhang, W. Che, and Bing Qin. 2015. Transition-based syntactic linearization. In *NAACL 2015*, pages 113–122.

N. McKinley and S. Ray. 2014. A decision-theoretic approach to natural language generation. In *ACL 2014*, volume 52, pages 14–1052.

T. Mikolov, I. Sutskever, K. Chen, G. S. Corrado, and J. Dean. 2013. Distributed representations of words and phrases and their compositionality. In *NIPS 2013*, pages 3111–3119.

D. Okanohara and J. Tsujii. 2007. A discriminative language model with pseudo-negative samples. In *ACL 2007*, volume 45, pages 73–80.

V. Rieser and O. Lemon. 2009. Natural language generation as planning under uncertainty for spoken dialogue systems. In *EACL 2009*, pages 683–691.

D. Silver, A. Huang, C. J. Maddison, A. Guez, L. Sifre, G. Driessche, J. Schrittwieser, I. Antonoglou, V. Panneershelvam, M. Lanctot, S. Dieleman, D. Grewe, J. Nham, N. Kalchbrenner, I. Sutskever, T. Lillicrap, M. Leach, K. Kavukcuoglu, T. Graepel, and D. Hassabis. 2016. Mastering the game of go with deep neural networks and tree search. *Nature*, 529:484–489.

R. S. Sutton and A. G. Barto. 1998. Reinforcement learning: An introduction. *MIT Press*.

T. Wen, M. Gašić, N. Mrkšić, P. Su, D. Vandyke, and S. Young. 2015. Semantically conditioned lstm-based natural language generation for spoken dialogue systems. In *EMNLP 2015*, pages 1711–1721.

M. J. Zaki. 2002. Efficiently mining frequent trees in a forest. In *KDD 2002*, volume 8, pages 71–80.

Empirical Determination of Basic Heuristics for Narrative Content Planning

Pablo Gervás
Instituto de Tecnología del Conocimiento
Universidad Complutense de Madrid
Ciudad Universitaria, 28040 Madrid, Spain
`pgervas@ucm.es`

Abstract

Stories are sequential in nature but they are used to package human experience that involves many things happening at the same time, to several people or in several locations. The mechanics of this packaging process constitute an instance of content planning that has not ben addressed in sufficient detail in existing NLG work. The present paper reviews a number of traditional stories in the light of the basic concepts of narratology that would be involved in the decisions involved in planning the content for tellings of these stories, proposes a number of basic principles to understand what is happening, and explores a possible way in which these principles may translate to basic heuristics for narrative content planning.

1 Introduction

Stories are a fundamental vehicle used by people to communicate and understand their environment. An interesting point is that, although stories are generally sequential in nature,[1] they are often used to package human experience that is, in its original form, anything but sequential. Complex sets of events involving many characters over many locations – which do not correspond to an ordered sequence of events but rather to a cloud of events that

---

[1] Stores are linear in the sense that there is only a single path through them, by reading the words and sentences in the order they appear in the page. Non-linear narratives – such as branching storylines, choose-your-own-adventure books or hypertext works – exist as cultural artifacts, but they do not share the importance that linear stories have as vehicles of human experience.

may overlap in time and space – are routinely converted into narrative discourse in the form of novels, short stories, or films. The mechanics of this process constitute the basic skill that novelists and film makers exhibit. Although there has been some debate as to whether writers first come up with a world and then tell about it or directly invent the story with the world being implicitly built during reading (Dehn, 1981) a computational model of the task involved in each of these options would be a useful tool. Work on cognitive models of writing has addressed the process of text composition, but these efforts focus on the elementary composition of text structure (Flower and Hayes, 1981) or the creativity affecting the ideas to be included (Sharples, 1999), rather than the story structure. Although these are worthy research topics, and there are a number of additional issues that are indeed significant from an psychological perspective, the mechanics that underlie the transcription processes involved may provide important insights on the composition processes.

Recent efforts in the field of natural language generation have addressed the formalization of the basic representational elements that are involved in these process (Gervás, 2012; Gervás, 2014) but have stopped short of identifying specific heuristics that might be involved in the process.

The present paper reviews a number of traditional stories in the light of the basic concepts of narratology that would be involved in the decisions involved in planning the content for tellings of these stories, proposes a number of basic principles to understand what is happening, and explores a possible way in which these principles may translate to basic heuris-

Proceedings of the INLG 2016 Workshop on Computational Creativity and Natural Language Generation, pages 19–26,
Edinburgh, September 2016. ©2016 Association for Computational Linguistics

tics for narrative content planning.

2 Related Work

The outlined programme requires the introduction of basic concepts of narratology and brief discussion of how they have been addressed in related studies.

2.1 Narrative

An important distinction is made in studying narrative between the content of a story as it would have taken place in the real world – or an imagined one – and the way that an author chooses to present it. The content of the story is exhaustive in detail and all of its ingredients is fixed in time and space. The way this content is presented by a given author involves selecting only particular aspects to mention, and telling those aspects in a particular linear order. There are several ways of understanding and referring to this distinction (see (Abbot, 1986) for details), but for simplicity we will refer to the exhaustive content as the *fabula* of the story and to the particular way of telling it as the *discourse* chosen for it.

This distinction forces the consideration of two different reference frames for time: the time in which events happened in the fabula – which we will refer to as *story time* –, and the point in the sequence of the discourse in which the corresponding events are mentioned – which we will refer to as *discourse time*. The way in which story time and discourse time differ, and the way in which they relate to one another is traditionally known as *chronology* (Abbot, 1986).

Discourse is linear and fabula usually is not. A fabula may involve a world where only one action takes place at a time, none of these actions overlaps with the next, and each action is immediately perceptible by an agent that was focusing on the preceding one. But such cases are extremely rare. More complex fabulae require discourse to break the telling of events that happen simultaneously into separate segments of discourse (sometimes known as *narrative threads*), where each thread follows a different character as they go through different experiences over the same period of story time. This is known as *focalization* (Genette, 1980). When discourse needs to change focalizer to go back in time or go to a different location, these changes may need to be explicitly marked as contexualizations of the new thread with respect to the preceding one, in order to help the reader make the correct interpretation (Gervás, 2014).

2.2 Narrative Planning in Natural Language Generation

The mechanics that this paper sets out to clarify correspond to the particular instantiation of the *content planning* task (Reiter and Dale, 2000) for the case when the content to be conveyed is a fabula and the text to be generated is a discourse, in the sense described above. With respect to prior work in the field of NLG, the present paper focuses on the task described as *narrative planner* in Callaway's work on narrative prose generation (Callaway, 2002), which focused on narrative realization rather than narrative planning. It also correlates reasonably well with efforts to generate discourse to describe sports events (Lareau et al., 2011; Bouayad-Agha et al., 2011; Allen et al., 2010) if the events that took place in the corresponding games are considered the fabula. The present work addresses the task in more detail by considering aspects such as characters and protagonism. Also related is work on the automatic generation of cinematic visual discourse (Jhala and Young, 2010), which shares the goal of identifying the best linear sequence of restricted views to convey a given content (or fabula). Where cinematic visual discourse focuses on restricted views as determined but the part of a scene that can be covered by a camera take, the present paper focuses on restricted views as determined by focalization on a given character – and telling only what that character might have perceived.

A set of elementary data structures to capture some of the concepts of narrative composition as described in section 2.1 has been proposed in (Gervás, 2012; Gervás, 2014). This work introduced concepts of a *fibre* – the restricted view of a given fabula as perceived by a given focalizer character –, and the tasks of *heckling* a fabula into fibres and *splicing* a selection of those fibres into a single linear discourse.

```
 1  Mother pig tells boys to build
 2  Pig1 builds house of straw
 3  Pig2 builds house of sticks
 4  Pig3 builds house of bricks
 5  Wolf blows house of straw away
 6  Pig1 runs to house of sticks
 7  Wolf blows house of sticks away
 8  Pigs 1 & 2 run to house of bricks
 9  Wolf fails to blow house and leaves
10  Pigs and their mother rejoice
```

Table 1: Story of the Three Little Pigs

2.3 Narrative Planning in Cognitive Models of Writing

The classic model of the writing task from a cognitive point of view (Flower and Hayes, 1981) focuses on the production of informative documents, with little attention devoted to the particular case of narrative discourse. The work of (Sharples, 1999) addresses writing as a task of creative design, focusing on the interplay between following an initial set of constraints and revising those constraints as a result of reflection on partial results obtained during discourse production. Such a high-level abstract view of the process is clearly relevant for narrative generation, but the particular case of narrative discourse as considered here was not considered.

3 Empirical Study of How Known Stories are Planned

In order to understand how the mechanics of building a discourse for a given fabula operate, we turn to the analysis of two traditional stories. For each one, we try to infer what the fabula for the story might be, and correlate that with the discourse as we have come to know it. From his comparison, we hope to obtain insights on the decisions that need to be taken and the heuristics that may be employed to inform them.

3.1 The Three Little Pigs

The story of the Three Little Pigs (outlined in Table 1) provides an interesting example of how the process of content planning moves from a fabula to a discourse. In this case, the fabula would be a record of the activity of every character from the start of the story to the end. A sketch of this would correspond to the representation given in Figure 1a, which provides a graphical depiction of the fabula. Here you can follow all characters as they move around the story world and interact with one another. This representation is accurate but does not correspond to the version of the story that everybody knows. Because that corresponds to one possible discourse that "tells" this fabula. This discourse is captured in the representation given in Figure 1b. Rather than tell what happpens to all characters at each point in time, the discourse focuses on a small subset of the action – that perceived by the characters that are more relevant to the story at that point. Where the actions relevant to the story at a given time point occur too far apart to be perceived by the same characters, the discourse focuses first on one possible location, and then moves back in time to focus on a different location. An example of this occurs in the second time point of the story, where the discourse tells in sequence how each little pig builds a different house, even though all the houses are built over the same time period.

This corresponds to the traditional concept of focalization: at time point 2, the discourse focalises respectively on each of the three little pigs as they build their houses.

There are a number of additional interesting features to be observed in this story. First, there is a significant portion of the fabula that is not present in the discourse. The activity of the pig's mother from time point 1 – when she send off her sons into the world – to time point 9 – when she joins them to celebrate their survival –, the activity of little pigs number two and three from they build their own house to the time they are asked to harbour their harassed brothers fleeing from the wolf, or the activity of the wolf whenever he is not threatening the little pigs, are not covered by the discourse.

We have no way of knowing – from the story as it is traditionally told – whether nothing happens to these character over those periods of time. We can only infer that nothing happens to them that is relevant to the story. This is an important point that can later be translated into useful heuristics for content planning.

Two important issues can be pointed out. First, the story is about the three little pigs: other characters such as the mother or the wolf only come into the story as they interact with the main charac-

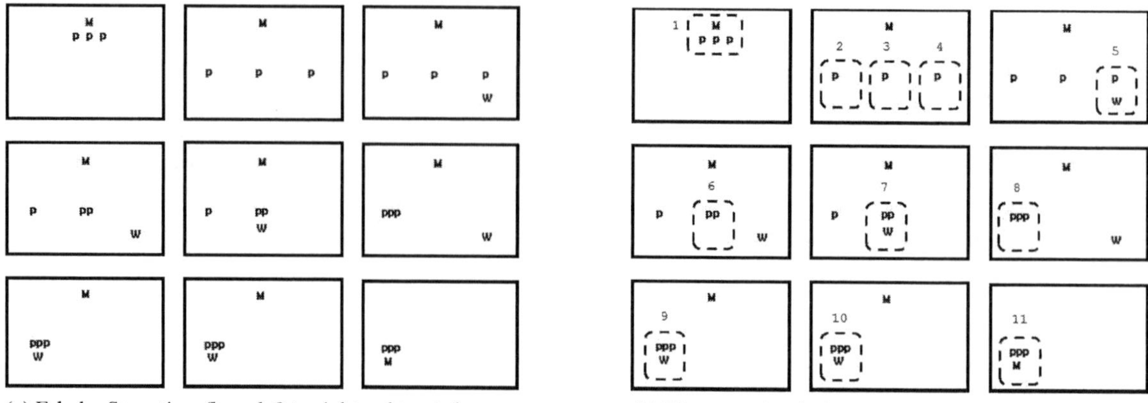

(a) Fabula. Story time flows left to right and top to bottom.

(b) Discourse (marked out over the fabula). Discourse time marked in Arabic numerals

Figure 1: Fabula and discourse for the story of the Three Little Pigs

```
 1   Mother send LRRH to Granny
 2   LRRH sets off through forest
 3   Wolf send LRRH on ``short cut''
 4   LRRH lingers to pick flowers
 5   Wolf reaches Granny first
 6   Wolf devours Granny
 7   LRRH arrives at Granny's
 8   Wolf devours LRRH
 9   Hunter arrives at Granny's
10   Hunter kills Wolf and victims emerge
```

Table 2: Story of the Little Red Riding Hood

ters. The discourse follows one or more of the pigs throughout the story. Second, even the main characters of the story may be ignored for a period of time if nothing relevant to the overall outcome is happening to them over that period.

3.2 Little Red Riding Hood

A similar analysis may be carried out for the story of Little Red Riding Hood (outlined in Table 2). Fabula and discourse for this story are shown in Figure 2. In this case, a larger set of different characters is involved, and the protagonist of the story is a single character, Little Red Riding Hood herself. The discourse indeed follows her most of the time – discourse segments 1 to 4, then briefly in 7, and finally in 10. But discourse segments 5 to 6 and 8 to 9 follow the wolf instead. This is a refinement to our previous analysis in that it introduces secondary characters that need to be followed over part of the time for the story of the protagonist to make sense. Here,

what happens to the wolf over the periods when the girl is not present is relevant to the story. This is because what happens to the wolf is partly shared with the girl and partly shared with characters that are closely related to the girl – the way in which wolf replaces the grandmother to then impersonate her in front of the girl. If this part of the fabula is not told, the story as seen from the point of view of the girl would not make sense. So the discourse needs to focalise on him over the periods where these events take place.

4   Identifying Abstract Principles from the Case Studies

The stories analysed above may be taken as evidence suggesting that a number of basic principles may be at play in the structuring of discourses from fabulas. Although the data set under consideration is cleary insufficient to draw any significant conclusions, a preliminary analysis of it may yield formative insights that can be used to construct baseline implementations of this task of narrative content planning or narrative composition.

An important point to consider is that any such principles would ideally be relevant not only for planning but also for interpreting narrative discourse. The interplay between interpretation and composition – with estimates of what a reader might interpret being used by writers to inform composition – has already been addressed as a plausible model in (Gervás and León, 2016), and tentative im-

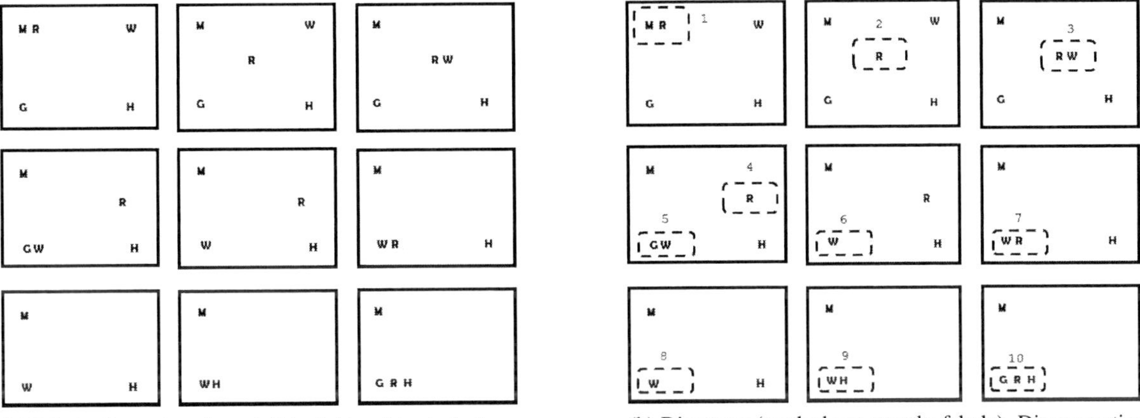

(a) Fabula. Story time flows left to right and top to bottom.
(b) Discourse (marked out over the fabula). Discourse time marked in Arabic numberals

Figure 2: Fabula and discourse for the story of Little Red Riding Hood

plementations were presented in (Gervás, 2014).

4.1 Basic Principles of Narrative Economy

The telling of stories is an instance of generic situation of communication involving a speaker, who tells the story, and an audience, who listens to the story. The audience may be made up of one or several listeners, and these may be specific people or a generic public. In all cases, the process as a whole is governed by a number of implicit assumptions that help speakers and listeners to optimise the processing required of them to take part. It would be helpful if we could identify some of these assumptions and formulate them as principles to govern our attempts to model human storytelling abilities. Such principles could be considered as particular instantiations of Gricean principles (Grice, 1975) governing exchanges between two agents.

When composing a story, a synthetic speaker may apply these principles to guide any decisions it needs to make. It would do so under the assumption that a listener (whether synthetic or authentic) would apply similar principles to the process of interpreting the resulting story. For the present purposes, we will focus on the case where there is a single listener. Extension to situations where there are multiple listeners may be considered as future work. Also, we consider principles applicable to a situation where a given fabula is available to the speaker and not available to the listener, and in which the goal for the listener to become aware of this fabula by inter-

preting a discourse based on it composed by speaker. The implicit task for the speaker is to construct the discourse that most economically satisfies this goal. The precise definition of economy may require further investigation, but some baseline definitions can be provided below.

The following basic principles may be postulated.

Principle of Focalized Perception: The listener will best understand a discourse describing a part of the fabula if it is phrased in terms of what a particular character might perceive.

Principle of Faithful Reporting: If the fabula contains an event involving a character that has already been mentioned in the discourse, that event should be mentioned in the discourse.

Principle of Temporal Congruity: The ordering of events as they appear in the discourse should follow as closely as possible the ordering of events in the fabula.

These principles have been stated at a high level of abstraction, but more pragmatic considerations may be derived from them. For instance, the Principle of Focalized Perception leads directly to the presentation of narrative discourse as a sequential combination of narrative threads – or fibres, in the terminiology proposed by (Gervás, 2014) – focalized on different characters. For the more traditional concepts of story, the focalizer for the most relevant thread in a given story can be considered the protagonist. This underlies the conventions applied by

23

both speakers and listeners in a basic storytelling situation. The Principle of Faithful Reporting is applied by speakers to optimise the length of the discourse by making no mention of certain characters when nothing is happening to them over long periods of time. The same principle is applied by listeners, allowing them to assume that if no action has been mentioned for a given character over a given period of time, that character has remained in the same conditions as it was when last mentioned. The Principle of Temporal Congruity is applied when encoding a temporal sequence, by allowing the speaker to simply enumerate the events on the assumption that, unless explicitly mentioned, the order of presentation matches with the order of occurrence. This reduces the need for temporal discourse markers or connectors to situations where divergences from this baseline occur. This generally happens when the discourse switches to a different narrative thread – which may require going back in time to where a different character was abandoned in favour of the focalizer of the thread that has just been reported – or sometimes when fragments from the same thread are presented in non-chronological order in the discourse (as in flashbacks or flashforwards on a given character).

4.2 Basic Heuristics for Content Planning

This reduced set of principles can now be used to produce a corresponding set of heuristics for narrative content planning.

A synthetic speaker faced with the task of constructing a discourse for a given fabula should:

1. identify the character in the fabula most likely to work as a protagonist

2. establish the narrative thread that focalises on this protagonist

3. for any additional characters – other than the protagonist – that appear in the resulting set of threads

    (a) identify points in the discourse where these characters suffer changes of state due to events that are not covered by the set of thread already included in the discourse

    (b) find the minimal span of narrative thread that would ensure coverage of those events if added to the discourse

    (c) splice this minimal span into the discourse

This heuristic-driven procedure is designed to operationalise the application of the stated principles as a reference baseline. They should lead to discourses that satisfy the principles in an elementary fashion, while requiring for their application no complex sources of knowledge. The relation between the procedure and the described principles is discussed below.

Points 1, 2 and 3.b arise from application of the Principle of Focalised Perception. Point 3.a is driven by the need to satisfy the Principle of Faithful Reporting. Point 3.c would need to take into consideration the Principle of Temporal Congruity either by inserting the additional span of narrative threads at a time of the discourse where the principle is satisfied, or by inserting additional temporal markers in the discourse to indicate where deviations from the expected chronology occurr.

4.3 Testing the Application of the Heuristics on the Studied Cases

The acceptability of the heuristic-driven procedure can be tested by checking that applying them to the known fabulae for the stories we have considered in detail does indeed lead to discourses that satisfy the basic principles. If the resulting discourses also match the known discourses for these stories this might be considered as reinforcement for the validity of these heuristics as a baseline.

The case of the Three Little Pigs is very basic if one allows for the three pigs to act collectively as protagonist. Then the story arises naturally from following them through the story, separating int different narrative threads when they split apart, rejoining when they meet again, and ordering the resulting thread spans according to the Principle of Temporal Congruity.

The case of Little Red Riding Hood can be discussed over the fabula and discourse presented in Figure 2. The valid choice for protagonist is the girl. Adding the thread for the girl to the draft discourse would result in a discourse covering discourse points 1, 2, 3, 4, 7 and 10. Application of point 3 of the heuristics would identify relevant events involving the grandmother, the wolf and the hunter that are not covered yet. Adding the thread of the wolf from fabula time point 4 to fabula time point 5 would cover all the events relevant to the grandmother and some of those by the wolf. Adding the thread for the grandmother would miss out fabula time point 5 – she has already been eaten by the wolf then – so this seems more economical. The events corresponding to discourse points 8 and 9 may covered by adding the thread for fabula time points 7 and 8 for either the wolf or the hunter. In each case, the choice results in a different result for discourse point 9, one focusing on the wolf and one on the hunter.

In both cases, the principles outlined are satisfied by the resulting discourses. The discourses also, within minimal variation generally match the known presentation of the stories.

5 Discussion

It is clear from the discussion above that there is more to narrative content planning than the elementary principles outlined so far. In the original story of Little Red Riding Hood, the span of thread to explain the presence of the wolf is not inserted into the discourse until it becomes apparent to the girl that she is not facing her grandmother. This seems to violate the principles as outlined. However, this type of operation may be considered as an exploitation of the principles by the speaker, where the explanation is withheld until the last possible moment, to enhance the surprise that it creates when it arrives.

Another important point to note is that the stories considered so far are very simple in nature, in as much as the additional spans that have to be inserted are very short. Further work is required to explore how principles such as those stated here might extend to more complex stories, where threads covering several time points need to be combined together. Specific principles would be required to govern how such longer threads are broken down into smaller fragments to allow focalization to switch back and forth between them over long time periods. This practice is well established, for instance, in TV series following multiple characters.

Regarding the relation with previous work, the principles and the heuristic-driven procedure outlined would be applicable in an implemented system for narrative composition such as the one described in (Gervás, 2014). They would rely on similar operations of heckling to identify the set of narrative threads corresponding to the fabula under consideration, and they would provide content specific guidance during the splicing process which is only generically described in the original description of the system.

With respect to efforts to generate discourse to describe sports events (Allen et al., 2010), the present paper addresses the task at a slightly lower level of detail in terms of how the fabula is described. Some of the techniques presented in (Lareau et al., 2011; Bouayad-Agha et al., 2011) may be employed to identify the equivalent of a fabula for a given sports event. In that case, the principles and the procedure outlined here could be applicable to the task of constructing a discourse for such a fabula.

The issue of identifying the correct order in which to present the events of a story has been addressed in detail in (Shimorina, 2016). This work differs from the issues discussed in the present paper in that it considers the input to have already the form of a sequence. In this way, it addresses the problem of ordering events in the discourse for a story more in terms of selecting possible relative orderings for a given already linearised discourse. The present paper tackles the problem from one step further back than this, and considers temporal ordering in the context of the problem of linearization and the selection of appropriate focalizers. With respect to the introduction of markers for temporal ordering, there should be some interaction between the strategic decisions of content planning and the tactical decisions of surface realization. This will be addressed in further work.

6 Conclusions and Further Work

The study of well-known stories in terms of the basic concepts of fabula and discourse highlights the importance of focalization and chronology as tools for content planning. Based on elementary insights extracted from this study, a number of basic principles have been postulated that would apply to the task of constructing an acceptable discourse from a given fabula. These principles have been operationalised into a heuristic-driven procedure for addressing the task planning the content for a discourse that adequately describes the given fabula. The given procedure results in discourses that satisfy the basic principles and roughly match with the discourses known for the stories that have been considered.

The principles and procedures described in this paper are a tentative initial approach to bring together the terminological and conceptual frameworks of narratology and natural language generation. The paper combines the narratological view of a story – as a narrative with a fabula, a discourse, and focalization and chronology establishing the relation between one and the other – and the NLG view of content that needs to be planned into a discourse. These two views describe the same operation but are very rarely combined into a single view of the problem. By bringing them together, this paper attempts to exploit the synergies that arise. A major contribution is the formulation of the problem in terms that are reasonably specific – events, state changes, characters, protagonism – that allow for broad interpretation in the context of possibly different empirical settings or natural language generation systems.

Three different further efforts beyond the work described here can be foreseen. First, larger number of existing stories should be studied for further insights into how their corresponding fabulae relate to the discourses used to convey them. It may also consider cases where more than one discourse is available for what is nominally the same story. This would allow consideration of explicit choices made by writers in creating the different versions of the discourse. Second, more complex stories, as outlined in section 5, should be considered, with a view to extending or refining the set of principles proposed here. Third, the procedure should be implemented in existing story generation systems to test its applicability over different representations of stories and specific domains.

References

S. Abbot. 1986. *Narrative*. Cambridge University Press.

N. D. Allen, J. R. Templon, P.S. McNally, L. Birnbaum, and K.Hammond. 2010. Statsmonkey: A data-driven sports narrative writer. In *Computational Models of Narrative: AAAI Fall Symposium 2010*.

N. Bouayad-Agha, G.Casamayor, and L. Wanner. 2011. Content selection from an ontology-based knowledge base for the generation of football summaries. In *Proc. ENLG 2011*, pages 72–81.

C. B. Callaway. 2002. Narrative prose generation. *Artificial Intelligence*, 139(2):213–252.

Natalie Dehn. 1981. Story generation after tale-spin. In Ann Drinan, editor, *Proceedings of the 7th international joint conference on artificial intelligence (IJCAI 1981), 24-28 August 1981*, pages 16–18, Menlo Park, CA, USA. AAAI.

L. Flower and J.R. Hayes. 1981. A cognitive process theory of writing. *College Composition and Communication*, 32(4):365–387.

G. Genette. 1980. *Narrative discourse : an essay in method*. Cornell University Press.

P. Gervás and C. León. 2016. Intgrating purpose and revision into a computational model of literary generation. In Mirko Degli Espositi, Eduardo G. Altmann, and François Pachet, editors, *Creativity and Universality in Language*. Springer.

P. Gervás. 2012. From the fleece of fact to narrative yarns: a computational model of narrative composition. In *Proc. Workshop on Computational Models of Narrative 2012*.

P. Gervás. 2014. Composing narrative discourse for stories of many characters: a case study over a chess game. *Literary and Linguistic Computing*, 29(4), 08/14.

H. P. Grice. 1975. Logic and conversation. In P. Cole and J. L. Morgan, editors, *Syntax and Semantics: Vol. 3: Speech Acts*, pages 41–58. Academic Press, San Diego, CA.

A. Jhala and R. M. Young. 2010. Cinematic visual discourse: Representation, generation, and evaluation. *IEEE Trans. on Comp. Int. and AI in Games*, 2(2):69–81.

F. Lareau, M. Dras, and R. Dale. 2011. Detecting interesting event sequences for sports reporting. In *Proc. ENLG 2011*, pages 200–205.

E. Reiter and R. Dale. 2000. *Building Natural Language Generation Systems*. Cambridge University Press.

M. Sharples. 1999. *How We Write: Writing As Creative Design*. Routledge, June.

A. Shimorina. 2016. Generating Stories from Different Event Orders: A Statistical Approach. Master's thesis, University of Malta, Malta.

Acknowledgments

This work was partially supported by FP7 projects WHIM (Grant Agreement 611560) and PROS-ECCO (Grant Agreement 600653).

X575: writing rengas with web services

Daniel Winterstein
Winterwell Associates
daniel@winterwell.com

Joseph Corneli
Goldsmiths College, University of London
j.corneli@gold.ac.uk

Abstract

Our software system simulates the classical collaborative Japanese poetry form, *renga*, made of linked haikus. We used NLP methods wrapped up as web services. This approach is suitable for collaborative human-AI generation, as well as purely computer-generated poetry. Evaluation included a blind survey comparing AI and human haiku. To gather ideas for future work, we examine related research in semiotics, linguistics, and computing.

1 Introduction

Computer haikus have been explored in practice at least since Lutz (1959). More recently, haikus have been used by Ventura (2016) as the testbed for a thought experiment on levels of computational creativity. As we will discuss below, the classic haiku traditionally formed the starting verse of a longer poetry jam, resulting in a poem called a *renga*. A computational exploration of renga writing allows us to return to some of the classical ideas in Japanese poetry via thoroughly modern ideas like concept blending and collaborative AI.

Ventura's creative levels range from *randomisation* to *plagiarisation*, *memorisation*, *generalisation*, *filtration*, *inception*[1] and *creation*. Further gradations and criteria could be advanced, for example, the fitness function used for filtration could be developed and refined as the system *learns*. Creativity

might be assessed in a social context, as we investigate how a system *collaborates*.

While self-play was a good way for the recently developed board game-playing system AlphaGo to transcend its training data (Silver et al., 2016), we do not yet have computationally robust qualitative evaluation measures for the poetry domain, where there is no obvious "winning condition." We began by creating a program for generating haikus, trained on a small corpus. Our technical aim then was to simulate the collaborative creation of renga, i.e., linked haikus. There are several forms of renga with varying constraints (Carley, 2015), for example the 20 stanza "Nijiun" renga which alternates between two-line and three-line verses, with a focus on seasonal symbolism and rules against repetition.[2] Our initial effort was a technical success, however the rengas we produced fail to fully satisfy classical constraints. A subsequent experiment is more convincing in this regard, but still leaves room for improvement. Our discussion considers the aesthetics of the generated poems and outlines directions for future research.

2 Background

Coleridge considered poetry to be "the blossom and the fragrance of all human knowledge." AI researcher Ruli Manurung defines poetry somewhat more drily: "A *poem* is a natural language artefact which simultaneously fulfils the properties of meaningfulness, grammaticality and poeticness" (Manurung, 2004, p. 8).

The *haiku* as we know it was originally called

---

[1] "[I]nject[ing] knowledge into a computationally creative system without leaving the injector's fingerprints all over the resulting artifacts."

[2] http://www.renga-platform.co.uk/webpages/renga_01.htm

Proceedings of the INLG 2016 Workshop on Computational Creativity and Natural Language Generation, pages 27–30,
Edinburgh, September 2016. ©2016 Association for Computational Linguistics

hokku – 発句, literally the "starting verse" of a collaboratively written poem, *hakai no renga*. Typically each of following links in a renga take the familiar 5/7/5 syllable form. Classical rengas vary in length from two to 100 links (and, rarely, even 1000). The starting verse is traditionally comprised of two images, with a *kireji* – a sharp cut – between them. The term *haiku* introduced by the 19th Century poet Masaoka Shiki supersedes the older term. Stylistically, a haiku captures a moment.

In classical renga, all of the verses after the first have additional complex constraints, such as requiring certain images to be used at certain points, but disallowing repetition, with various proximity constraints. The setting in which rengas were composed is also worth commenting on. A few poets would compose together in party atmosphere, with one honoured guest proposing the starting haiku, then the next responding, and continuing in turn, subject to the oversight of a scribe and a renga master. These poetry parties were once so popular and time consuming that they were viewed as a major decadence. Jin'Ichi et al. (1975) offers a useful overview.

Because of the way we've constructed our haiku generating system, it can take an entire haiku as its input topic – we just add the word vectors to make a topic model – and compose a response. This affords AI-to-AI collaboration, or AI-human collaboration. It can also blend two inputs – for example, the previous haiku and the current constraint from the renga ruleset (e.g., the requirement to allude to "cherry blossoms" or "the moon").

3 Implementation

Working with a small haiku corpus, we used a POS tagger to reveal the grammatical structure typical to haikus. The CMU Pronouncing Dictionary is used to count syllables of words that fill in this structure.[3] The Brown corpus was used to generate n-grams, and the generation process prefers more common constructions in haikus.[4] Wikipedia data was processed with GloVe (Pennington et al., 2014) to create a semantic vector space model of topics, based

on word co-occurrences.[5] Adding a web API turned the haiku generating system into a haiku server, and facilitated subsequent work with FloWr. In short:

```
1. Haiku corpus → POS tagger →
   grammatical skeleton fragments.
2. General text corpus → n-gram model.
3. Wiki corpus → topic vectors.
4. Combine skeleton fragments to make a
   haiku template.
5. Assign syllable counts to slots.
6. Fill in the template, preferring
   n-grams and close topic matches.
7. Wrap the process with a JSON HTTP
   API
```

4 Experiments

I. Initial evaluation of haikus Following Manurung's definition of poetry, above, we would like to assess: (1) whether a given haiku makes sense and how well it fits the topic, (2) whether it fits the form, i.e., is it a valid haiku?, and (3), the beauty of the writing, the emotion it evokes. Details of a survey-based blind comparison of human and computer-written haikus were written up by Aji (2015). The system was then extended with multiple inputs, in some cases producing interesting blends: e.g., the following in response to "frog pond" and "moon":

> *that gull in the dress –*
> *vivacious in statue*
> *from so many ebbs*

II. Generation of rengas Here are two rengas generated by wrapping the haiku API inside the FloWr flowchart system (Charnley et al., 2016):

fertile forefingers	*that vase in the quilt –*
took orchard for my lather	*the effeminate of names*
brackish was cherished	*with a colored juice*
toddler of strong bet	*cases of sibyl*
foaling feels to a good tooth	*and a stylish curators*
thriving like a paw	*from downed in the aim*
a drawer straight inside	*figures of digress*
under the slicked interim	*and a sumac excises*
to shrink the safe cute	*from key in the ribbed*
readjusted blots	*cluster for icebergs –*
in the creativity –	*and a waging everglades*
one child at a love	*from huge in the drug*

In each case, the prompt for the first link is "flower blossom" and each link is passed on to

---

[3]`http://www.speech.cs.cmu.edu/cgi-bin/cmudict`

[4]`https://en.wikipedia.org/wiki/Wikipedia:Database_download`

[5]`http://nlp.stanford.edu/projects/glove/`

the next link along with a secondary prompt. The secondary links are "moon," "autumn," and "love," respectively. For the first renga, we designed a flowchart that selects the "most positive" haiku from the ten that the haiku API returns, using the AFINN word list.[6] In the second renga, we designed a flowchart to select the haiku with the lowest word variety (computed in terms of Levenshtein distance).

III. Tuning the parameters for the Nijiun form

national forces
on the government afghan
because no-one armed

military government
the war on the armed
afghan

a soviet troops
upcoming in the winter
military armed

troops fighting military
in the administration

blooms operations
the military planted
of the flower war

the army of government
we die the war civilians

We made improvements to the use of the Brown corpus to utilise n-grams for word-flow and sense, as well as tuning the weightings given to sense and topic. We implemented the injection of topics via by blending, as per classical constraints (e.g., required seasonal themes like "winter," or "flowers" in the penultimate link). At left, we quote the closing links of the first Nijiun renga generated by our software.

5 Discussion and Related Work

Towards automated evaluation Some aspects of the evaluation dimensions are built into the way the poems are constructed.

Form: the haiku-generating subsystem guarantees that the requirements of a grammatical skeleton are met, and the 5/7/5 syllable pattern is guaranteed (up to the accuracy of the CMU Pronouncing Dictionary). Surface form scales up well for rengas.

Sense: the haiku generating subsystem uses an n-gram model of text likelihood, which will yield a higher score for constructions that match frequently observed phrases. In our first round of experiments with rengas, sense tended to degrade quickly. Our subsequent adaptations to the renga generation algorithm prioritise greater continuitity between links.

Topic: we used a vector model of the topic word(s), and can measure the distance to the vector given by the sum of the words in the poem.

[6] http://neuro.imm.dtu.dk/wiki/AFINN

Emotion: In our experiment with FloWr, we used a quite simple method, filtering a list for the "most positive" haikus. Mohammad (2016) surveys more recent work in NLP on modelling emotion, which could be exploited in future work.

Beauty: Waugh (1980) points out that language is based on a "hierarchy of signs ... of ascending complexity, but also one of ascending freedom or creativity," and also remarks that a "poem provides its own 'universe of discourse.'" To some extent these criteria pull in opposite directions: towards complexity, and towards coherence, respectively. Our first rengas could not be reasonably described as a 'universe of discourse' but rather, a 'universe of random nonsense'. This is improved in the subsequent experiment. Traditional rengas forbid repetition, and discourage overt reflection on themes like death, war, illness, impermanence, religion and sex (Carley, 2015). Thus, despite being coherent, the repetitive "military" theme in the final example above is not appropriate to classical constraints. A reader may identify some fortuitous resonances, e.g., "the flower war" is interesting within the "afghan" context established in earlier links – but the system itself does not yet recognise these features.

Some paths forward Wiggins and Forth (2015) use hierarchical models in a system that builds a formative evaluation as it composes or reads sentences, judging how well they match learned patterns. While this seems to have more to do with constraints around typicality, per Waugh, there is room for creativity within hierarchies. Hoey (2005) makes a convincing argument that satisfying lexical constraints while violating some familiar patterns may come across as interesting and creative.

Word similarities can be found using GloVe: this would presumably produce links with more coherent meanings, compared to the edit distance-based measure we used. Ali Javaheri Javid et al. (2016) use *information gain* to model the aesthetics of cellular automata. Can these ideas be combined to model evolving topic salience, complexity, and coherence?

If the system provided a *razo* (the troubadours' jargon for "rationale"; see Agamben (1999, p. 79)), we could debug that, and perhaps involve additional AI systems in the process (Corneli et al., 2015).

6 Conclusion

In terms of Ventura's hierarchy of creative levels, the haiku system appears to be in the "generalisation" stage. Our renga-writing experiments with FloWr brought in a "filtration" aspect. The research themes discussed above point to directions for future work in pursuit of the "inception" and "creativity" stages.

Some previous work with haiku, e.g. Netzer et al. (2009) and Rzepka and Araki (2015), have addressed the problem of *meaning*. The renga form brings these issues to the fore. We hope this early work has motivated further interest in this challenging and enjoyable poetic form that – like other less constrained forms of dialogue – combines themes of natural language generation and understanding. One natural next step would be a series of experiments in collaborative human-AI generation of rengas. Our haiku software is available for future experiments.[7]

Acknowledgement

This research was supported by the Future and Emerging Technologies (FET) programme within the Seventh Framework Programme for Research of the European Commission, under FET-Open Grant number 611553 (COINVENT).

References

Giorgio Agamben. 1999. *The end of the poem: Studies in poetics*. Stanford University Press.

Alham Fikri Aji. 2015. Automated haiku generation based on word vector models. Master's thesis. University of Edinburgh.

Mohammad Ali Javaheri Javid, Tim Blackwell, Robert Zimmer, and Mohammad Majid al Rifaie. 2016. Analysis of information gain and Kolmogorov complexity for structural evaluation of cellular automata configurations. *Connection Science*, 28(2):155–170.

John Carley. 2015. *Renku Reckoner*. Darlington Richards Press.

John Charnley, Simon Colton, Maria Teresa Llano, and Joseph Corneli. 2016. The FloWr Online Platform: Automated Programming and Computational Creativity as a Service. In Amílcar Cardoso, François Pachet, Vincent Corruble, and Fiammetta Ghedini, editors, *Proceedings of the Seventh International Conference on Computational Creativity, ICCC 2016*.

Joseph Corneli, Anna Jordanous, Rosie Shepperd, Maria Teresa Llano, Joanna Misztal, Simon Colton, and Christian Guckelsberger. 2015. Computational poetry workshop: Making sense of work in progress. In S. Colton, H. Toivonen, M. Cook, and D. Ventura, editors, *Proceedings of the Sixth International Conference on Computational Creativity, ICCC 2015*.

Michael Hoey. 2005. *Lexical priming: A new theory of words and language*. Psychology Press.

Konishi Jin'Ichi, Karen Brazell, and Lewis Cook. 1975. The Art of Renga. *Journal of Japanese Studies*, pages 29–61.

Theo Lutz. 1959. Stochastische texte. *Augenblick*, 4(1):3–9.

Hisar Maruli Manurung. 2004. *An evolutionary algorithm approach to poetry generation*. Ph.D. thesis. University of Edinburgh.

Saif M. Mohammad. 2016. Sentiment Analysis: Detecting Valence, Emotions, and Other Affectual States from Text. In Herb Meiselman, editor, *Emotion Measurement*. Elsevier.

Yael Netzer, David Gabay, Yoav Goldberg, and Michael Elhadad. 2009. Gaiku: Generating haiku with Word Associations Norms. In Anna Feldman and Birte Loenneker-Rodman, editors, *Proceedings of the Workshop on Computational Approaches to Linguistic Creativity*, pages 32–39. ACL.

Jeffrey Pennington, Richard Socher, and Christopher D. Manning. 2014. GloVe: Global Vectors for Word Representation. In *Empirical Methods in Natural Language Processing (EMNLP)*, pages 1532–1543.

Rafal Rzepka and Kenji Araki. 2015. Haiku Generator That Reads Blogs and Illustrates Them with Sounds and Images. In *Proceedings of the 24th International Conference on Artificial Intelligence*, pages 2496–2502. AAAI Press.

David Silver, Aja Huang, Chris J Maddison, Arthur Guez, Laurent Sifre, George Van Den Driessche, Julian Schrittwieser, Ioannis Antonoglou, Veda Panneershelvam, Marc Lanctot, et al. 2016. Mastering the game of Go with deep neural networks and tree search. *Nature*, 529(7587):484–489.

Dan Ventura. 2016. Mere Generation: Essential Barometer or Dated Concept? In Amílcar Cardoso, François Pachet, Vincent Corruble, and Fiammetta Ghedini, editors, *Proceedings of the Seventh International Conference on Computational Creativity, ICCC 2016*.

Linda R Waugh. 1980. The poetic function in the theory of Roman Jakobson. *Poetics Today*, 2(1a):57–82.

Geraint A Wiggins and Jamie Forth. 2015. IDyOT: a computational theory of creativity as everyday reasoning from learned information. In *Computational Creativity Research: Towards Creative Machines*, pages 127–148. Springer.

---

[7] `https://github.com/winterstein/HaikuGen`

A Challenge to the Third Hoshi Shinichi Award

Satoshi Sato

Graduate School of Engineering

Nagoya University

Furo-cho, Chikusa, Nagoya, 464-8603, JAPAN

ssato@nuee.nagoya-u.ac.jp

Abstract

We produced two stories by using a computer program and submitted them to the third Hoshi Shinichi Award, a Japanese literary award open to non-humans as well as humans. This paper reports what system we implemented for the submission and how we made the stories by using the system.

1 Introduction

On September 2015. We produced two stories by using a computer program and submitted them to the third Hoshi Shinichi Award, a Japanese literary award.

> The clouds hung low that day in an overcast sky. Inside, though, the temperature and humidity were perfectly controlled. Yoko was sitting lazily on the couch, passing the time playing pointless games. (Parry, 2016).

This is an English translation of the very beginning of a story titled "コンピュータが小説を書く日 (The day a computer writes a novel)." Another story is titled "私の仕事は (My Job)", which contains a dialogue including the following utterance of a character.

> "Did you hear yesterday's news? About jobs being cut, as cheap, clever humanoid robots are replacing humans?" (Parry, 2016).

Table 1: Number of Stories in 3rd Hoshi Shinichi Award

	Adult	Student (U-26)	Junior (U-16)
submitted	1449	349	763
1st screening	n/a	n/a	n/a
2nd screening	n/a	n/a	n/a
3rd screening	16	11	15
final (awarded)	6	3	5

The Hoshi Shinichi Award, started on 2013, has an unusual feature: It is open to non-humans as well as humans. The only requirement is that the text should be written in Japanese limited in ten thousand characters. The length roughly corresponds to four thousand words in English.

Table 1 shows the statistics of the third Hoshi Shinichi Award[1]. The award had three divisions: Adult, Student (under 26 years old), and Junior (junior high school students or younger children). The screening process consisted of four rounds, where author information was not informed to judges. It finally selected stories for awards including *grand prix* in each division.

The official of the Hoshi Shinichi Award disclosed that eleven stories among 2,561 received stories were written with some help of computer programs. Four stories among above eleven are open to the public by their authors: two stories created by the AIWolf project[2], and other two by our team. The official also disclosed that one of these four stories passed the first round of the screening process.

---

[1]http://hoshiaward.nikkei.co.jp

[2]http://aiwolf.org

Proceedings of the INLG 2016 Workshop on Computational Creativity and Natural Language Generation, pages 31–35,
Edinburgh, September 2016. ©2016 Association for Computational Linguistics

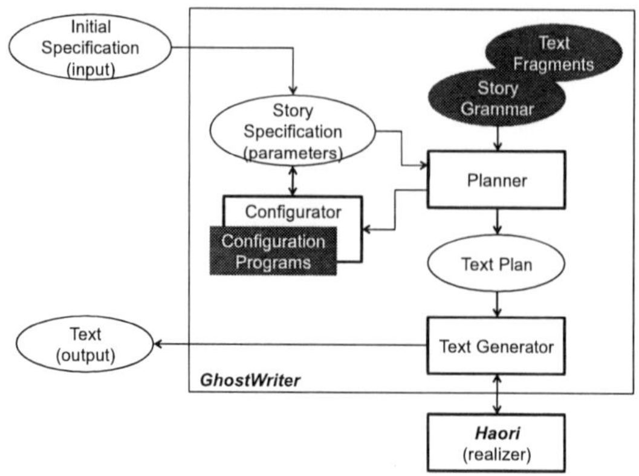

Figure 1: The GhostWriter system

The strategies of two teams were completely opposite. The AIWolf team automated plot generation. They used a log of Werewolf game played by AI programs as a plot (i.e., story outline), and a human researcher wrote a story based on it. In contrast, our team automated text generation. We first prepared several components needed for generating stories such as a story grammar and a set of text fragments, and then our system constructed a story (text) automatically using these components, which we submitted without any modification.

We believe that the first sub-goal to achieve is to generate stories that are imperceptible as computer-generated to readers. Our purpose of this submission was to know whether current generation technologies reach this sub-goal.

2   The GHOSTWRITER System

To automate text generation, we implemented a system named GHOSTWRITER. Figure 1 shows the architecture of the system. The system consists of three modules: planner, configurator, and text generator. For practical text generation, the system also requires three types of knowledge component: a story grammar, a set of text fragments, and a set of configuration programs. Among them, the story grammar is the primal knowledge component.

2.1   Planner and Configurator

The story grammar is an augmented context-free grammar, where a story outline is encoded. In this grammar, a nonterminal symbol corresponds to a certain textual unit such as section, paragraph, and

sentence; a terminal corresponds to an internal representation of a certain text fragment, typically sentence or clause.

From a start nonterminal symbol, a grammar non-deterministically produces a derivation tree, which represents a concrete text structure enough to produce the corresponding surface string. That is what we call *text plan*. In GHOSTWRITER, text planning is just derivation by a story grammar.

A grammar is *augmented*; it means that a nonterminal symbol can take a bundle of parameters. During derivation, these parameters can convey any information from a nonterminal symbol to others, and also can control rule application. Through these parameters, a story specification is delivered into a grammar.

The input of story generation is a three-tuple: a story grammar, a start nonterminal symbol, and an initial specification (a bundle of parameters) given to the start nonterminal for derivation. The last one can be empty, which we will see later.

Suppose the following story grammar is defined.

Beginning → descDay descRoom descChar
descDay → *"describe the day with the weather"*
descRoom → *"describe the room status"*
descChar → *"describe the owner of the room"*

The first rule says that the Beginning section consists of three components. The other rules are terminated rules, each of which produces a terminal, an internal representation of a text fragment.

Each nonterminal symbol *knows* what parameters are required for derivation. For example, a nonterminal descDay knows that a parameter `weather` is required. If the value of `weather` is given or already determined, the rule is applied and then the weather description is produced as a terminal. If not, the configurator is called for determining the value of the parameter before rule application.

The body of the configurator is a set of configuration programs, each of which is specific to a parameter. For example, the `weather` configuration program determines the value of `weather` by selecting one of five possible weather choices, such as *fine*, *hot*, *cloudy*, *rainy*, and *windy*. In general, a value is determined depending on several related parameters to keep the story consistent. For example, the parameter `roomStatus`, required for the derivation of descRoom, is determined depending on the values of `isOwnerInRoom?` and `weather`. If the owner is in the room and the weather is hot, the value takes, for example, "the air-conditioner is working".

If we prepare a configuration program for every parameter, the system can produce a derivation tree from the empty setting. In this case, the system determines all parameters required for the derivation automatically.

A grammar is nondeterministic. A rule is selected at random among applicable ones and a backtracking mechanism is implemented to break a deadlock. In contrast, the configurator works deterministically in the current implementation, so the order of determining parameters has to be carefully designed and implemented not to reach a deadlock.

2.2 Text Generator

The text generator produces a text string from a text plan, i.e, a derivation tree, by concatenating strings produced from terminals. Each terminal is an internal representation of a certain text fragment that a surface realizer HAORI accepts.

HAORI is a relatively simple surface realizer (Reiter and Dale, 2000), which is responsible for selection of functional words (particles) and conjugation. As far as we know, there was no Japanese surface realizer before HAORI, so we designed and implemented it for this challenge.

3 Development of Knowledge Components

As mentioned before, the system requires three knowledge components for a particular type of story: a story grammar, a set of text fragments, and a set of configuration programs. The development of these components is not automated at all.

The actual procedure that we took was as follows.

1. Write a sample story that the system should generate.

2. Decompose the story into several parts and apply this recursively. As a result, the story structure (text plan) is obtained.

3. Write rules and text fragments that are required to generate the text plan. After we finish this step, the system can generate the sample story.

4. Write replacements of rules and text fragments in order to enlarge text variations that system can generate.

5. Introduce parameters that control rule application and content (text-fragment) selection.

6. Write configuration programs for parameters to keep the story consistent.

7. Go to step 4 for further enrichment.

More replacements we write, more variations the system can generate. A replacement of upper level rule brings a global variation; a replacement of lower level rule or text fragment brings a local variation.

The story grammar of "The day a computer writes a novel" has only one top-level rule, which constructs a story from four parts. The first three are a series of three episodes, which are produced by the same sub-grammar. The size of this sub-grammar is: 53 nonterminals, 71 terminals, and 99 rules with 20 parameters. Each episode, which is written from the first-person (an AI program) perspective, consists of four sections: opening, description of his/her dissatisfaction with a current situation, description of a trigger to write a novel, and description of his/her absorption in writing. Typical length of an episode is 33 sentences.

After three episodes, the closing comes. The closing has two English translations.

> The day a computer wrote a novel. The computer, placing priority on the pursuit of its own joy, stopped working for humans. (Yomiuri Shinbun, 2016)

> The day a computer wrote a novel! The computer, pursuing its own rapture, gave up serving humans. (Parry, 2016)

This is a good example of local variations that we realized by our system.

4 Discussion

Our two stories were generated by using GHOST-WRITER, with different knowledge components. This fact shows that the system offers a general framework of story generation and can generate other types of story by replacing the knowledge components. In our case, the effort required to develop knowledge components was about a month per story.

Our stories are over 2,000 characters (around 100 sentences) in length. In order to obtain this length, we made a story as a series of episodes with the same structure. Another reason why we took this strategy is that this is a demonstration that a single grammar can generate different texts. In the case of "The day a computer writes a novel", the grammar can generate more than 1,000 different episodes and more than a million different stories. (Note that the variations of the second and the third episodes are restricted by the precedent episode(s) to avoid the duplication of, for example, characters.)

The maximum length of the Hoshi Shinichi Award is 10,000 characters, so the length of our stories is still short. At the conference on March 21, 2016, where we explained how we made the stories to the public, a professional novelist said that there is little chance to pass the screening process for such short stories and advised us to submit longer (i.e., around 10,000 characters) ones next time.

Probably these longer stories can be generated by using our current framework, but much more effort is necessary. In order to reduce the effort, we need a new mechanism that produces descriptions of characters, situations, and events with less preparation, because richer descriptions of such entities become more important in longer stories. A method to realize it is to construct a description database, which has a large number of typical example descriptions and modification ability, and accepts abstract commands such as "produce a literary description of a rainy day."

In addition, we need to enhance dialogue generation to make each utterance show speaker's characteristics. Note that a core part of each episode of "My Job" is a dialogue between two characters, automatic utterance characterization, however, was not implemented.

The story "The day a computer writes a novel" is written from the first-person (an AI program) perspective, as we mentioned before. There is a gender parameter of the first-person and it controls gender-specific expressions. The selection of gender-specific expressions should be executed by the text generator, however it was executed by the planner because HAORI did not have *a author* parameter to select author-specific word/expression selection.

The Hoshi Shinichi Award is a literary award where just one submitted story is evaluated. It is not an evaluation of story generators. We should note that, from a single generated story, we cannot evaluate the ability of the story generator, because a simple random generator may produce an amazing story; the probability is more than zero. Even if a generated story receives an award, this does not prove directly that the program is competitive or superior to human writers.

The crucial weak point of story generation research is that there is no mechanical method of evaluation: no method to determine a given text can be seen as story; no method to determine which story is better among a given set of stories. This is because story understanding is far from the current text understanding technology.

In this challenge, we focused on text generation (i.e., how to write), not on plot generation (i.e., what to write), although we had noticed that plot generation is the mainstream of story generation research (Meehan, 1981; Turner, 1994; Bringsjord and Ferrucci, 2000; Gervás, 2009). We believe that nobody wants to read a poor text just serialized an event sequence and such texts are easily perceived as machine-generated. That is why we placed text generation above plot generation.

Finally, I mention a project named "The whimsical AI project: I am a writer[3]", headed by Hitoshi Matsubara. The goal of this project is to produce new short stories as Shinichi Hoshi wrote. I am a member of this project and take charge of text generation. Story analysis and plot generation are also studied by other members.

5   Conclusion

This paper reported our challenge to the third Hoshi Shinichi Award. Our purpose of this challenge was to submit stories that were not imperceptible as computer-generated to readers. We have concluded that this purpose was achieved, based on comments

---

[3] The name of the project comes from the two titles of famous short stories written by Shinichi Hoshi: "きまぐれロボット (The Whimsical Robot)" and "殺し屋ですのよ (I am a killer)". http://www.fun.ac.jp/ kimagure_ai/

from professional novelists and audience at the conference on March 21.

We have opened a demonstration of generating stories at http://kotoba.nuee.nagoya-u.ac.jp/sc/gw/. Full text of submitted stories can be download from this web page. A video of demonstration can be seen at https://youtu.be/5dpJSzn5L4U.

Acknowledgments

Three students contributed to this work. The story "私の仕事は (My Job)" was created by Daiki Takagi and Ryohei Matsuyama. A part of HAORI was implemented by Kento Ogata. This work was supported by JSPS KAKENHI Grant Number 15H02748.

References

Selmer Bringsjord and David A. Ferrucci. 2000. *Artificial Intelligence and Literary Creativity*. Lawrence Erlbaum Associates, Inc. Publishers.

Pablo Gervás. 2009. Computational approaches to storytelling and creativity. *AI Magazine*, 30(3):49–62.

James Meehan. 1981. TAIL-SPIN. In Roger C. Schank and Christopher K. Riesbeck, editors, *Inside Computer Understanding: Five Programs Plus Miniatures*, pages 197–226. Psychology Press.

Richard Lloyd Parry. 2016. Robot commended by literary judges after 'writing' short story. Article of The Australian on March 24. http://www.theaustralian.com.au/news/world/the-timcs/robot-commended-by-literary-judges-after-writing-short-story/news-story/064b8d5e457b0322f6a58b54e1c33e3c.

Ehud Reiter and Robert Dale. 2000. *Building Natural Language Generation Systems*. Cambridge University Press.

Scott R. Turner. 1994. *The Creative Process: A Computer Model of Storytelling and Creativity*. Psychology Press.

Yomiuri Shinbun. 2016. AI-written novel passes literary prize screening. Article of The Japan News on March 23. http://the-japan-news.com/news/article/0002826970.

A Note on コンピュータが小説を書く日

The story, "The day a computer writes a novel", consists of three episodes and the closing. The outline of each episode is: An AI program, who is dissatisfied with a current situation, starts writing a novel with a trigger, and becomes absorbed in writing. This outline is hard-coded in the grammar. The major parameters are: AI (ability and gender), novel (integer sequence), current status (busy or nothing to do), trigger (for fun, reading a novel, or reading two novels), owner of AI (Yoko/female, Shinichi/male, or none), what to advise the owner (dressing, business, or love). These parameters control the instantiation of the outline, so they are determined before derivation of the episode. Other minor parameters effect contents and text realization within a local unit.

There is no official translation of the story. However, unofficial and partial translations in English, Korean, and Chinese are on the Web.

Automatic Modification of Communication Style in Dialogue Management

Louisa Pragst[1], Juliana Miehle[1], Stefan Ultes[2], Wolfgang Minker[1]
[1] Institute of Communications Engineering, Ulm University, Germany
{firstname.lastname}@uni-ulm.de
[2] Engineering Department, University of Cambridge, UK
su259@cam.ac.uk

Abstract

In task-oriented dialogues, there is often only one right answer the system can give. However, a lack of variation can seem repetitive and unnatural. Humans change the way they express something, e.g. by being more or less concise. We aim to approximate this ability by automatically varying the level of verbosity and directness of a given system action. In this work, we illustrate how verbosity and directness may be utilised in adaptive dialogue management and present different approaches to automatically generate varying levels of verbosity and directness for given system actions. Thereby, new and unforeseen system actions can be created dynamically.

1 Introduction

In a dialogue system, the Dialogue Management (DM) is responsible for selecting the system's next action, thereby shaping the flow of the conversation between human and computer. To this end, all possible system actions that can be executed are defined in advance. The definition of system actions requires diligence. Each system action needs to be foreseen and included. If an action is not foreseen in advance the resulting dialogue system is unable to react adequately. Adaptive DM puts even higher requirements on the definition of system actions as suitable possibilities for adaptation have to be provided in addition to the elementary dialogue flow.

One possibility for adaptation is changing the way information is communicated. Pragst (2015) shows that the level of verbosity and directness (in the following summarised as Communication Style (CS)) has a situation-dependent influence on the user's assessment of the dialogue. By automatically generating CS variants of system actions, the potential for adaptivity is increased without additional work during the definition of system actions. Furthermore, new and unforeseen system actions can be created by the system without human interference.

In this paper, we introduce approaches for the automatic generation of CS variants of system actions. We present CSs suitable for adaptive DM and discuss their applicability. Furthermore, we show how new system actions can be generated automatically by changing the CS of existing system actions.

The remainder of the paper is structured as follows: in Section 2, related work is introduced and put in relation to the work at hand. Subsequently, we introduce the CSs that are targeted for the automatic generation, namely verbosity and directness. Section 4 provides examples for the application of CS in adaptive DM. In Section 5, we introduce the architecture of our system and in Section 6, we give an overview over the utilised corpus. Our approach to the automatic generation of variations of system actions is presented in Section 7. Finally, we draw a conclusion and propose future work in Section 8.

2 Related Work

Adaptive DM has been in the focus of researchers for a long time. Hence, a number of adaptive DM architectures exists, e.g. (Gnjatović and Rösner, 2008; Ultes and Minker, 2014; Rieser and Lemon, 2011). Adaptation of the dialogue strategy to culture (Aylett and Paiva, 2012; Mascarenhas et al., 2013) as well as emotion (André et al., 2004; Gnja-

36

Proceedings of the INLG 2016 Workshop on Computational Creativity and Natural Language Generation, pages 36–40,
Edinburgh, September 2016. ©2016 Association for Computational Linguistics

tović and Rösner, 2008; Pittermann and Pittermann, 2007), among many others, has been implemented. While such architectures provide the means to execute an adaptive dialogue strategy, they rely on predefined system actions to provide a variety of system actions for adaptation.

In the area of language generation, paraphrasing is a major field of research and a lot of approaches for automating paraphrasing have been discussed, e.g. (Kozlowski et al., 2003; Langkilde and Knight, 1998). While this research addresses the generation of variations in the language output with the same semantic content, we focus on variations of the semantic content of a system action.

There have been efforts to model dialogue flows automatically, e.g (Beveridge and Fox, 2006; Niraula et al., 2014; Zhai and Williams, 2014; Kadlec et al., 2015). Their focus lies on the automatic extraction of complete dialogue flows and is strictly task-oriented. While in some of those examples system actions are extracted automatically, those system actions are reproductions. Also, no variants are provided as those would be unnecessary to solve a task. In contrast, we aim to enable our system to generate new ways to express the same semantics and thereby create possibilities for adaptation.

3 Introducing the Communication Styles

The CSs we take into account for realising adaptivity in DM stem from the Communication Sciences. In this paper, we address the level of verbosity and directness as they are feasible for adaptation to the user's situation (Pragst, 2015). We present their origins and a short description in the following.

Verbosity as CS is derived from Kaplan's description of cultural thought patterns (Kaplan, 1966) which refer to the way arguments are presented in written text. Amongst others, the thought patterns can be distinguished by the amount of information that is provided. The fact that different amounts of information are preferred by different cultures is also reported by Feghali (1997). Unnecessary information can be distracting from the main message to people accustomed to other thought patterns.

Regarding directness, Feghali (1997) observes that in some cultures it is favoured and expected to directly express your intent, while others prefer a more indirect CS whereby the listener has to deduce the intent from the context. In such cultures, directness can even be perceived as aggressive. An example for different levels of directness is saying either 'Take an aspirin.' or 'People often use aspirin when they have a headache.'

4 Application in Dialogue

Considering their origin as CS variants of different cultures, verbosity and directness are suitable choices for adaptation to the user's culture. Here, we present further application scenarios.

4.1 User Situation

It can be useful to include unrequested information in a system action. Useful background knowledge may be provided and an indirect CS can help to keep the user focused on the conversation as their constant attention is required to grasp the context.

However, in critical situations, e.g. if the user is driving, distracting them should be avoided. This may be achieved by being concise. Similarly, direct, unambiguous system actions do not have to be interpreted and thereby decrease the cognitive load.

The level of directness and verbosity was shown to be feasible as means of adaptation to the user situation by Pragst (2015).

4.2 User Emotion

Several studies indicate that adaptation to the user emotion can improve the user experience (e.g. (Bertrand et al., 2011)). CS may be a suitable mean to implement such adaptation.

A sad user may benefit from a system communicating in their culture's style as it provides a sense of familiarity. An angry user may prefer concise and direct system actions, because they are unwilling to listen to lengthy statements. This of course is also influenced by the user's culture. If direct statements are perceived as aggressive, they will likely disgruntle the user even more.

Considering the given examples, we are confident that CS is a suitable way to adapt the system behaviour to the user emotion.

4.3 System Emotion

Endowing emotion on a dialogue system can render the system more human-like and relatable. In addition to expressing the system emotion by modalities such as facial expression, it can be used in adaptive DM in order to provide system behaviour that is consistent with the system emotion. For example, anticipation might lead to concise, direct statements to avoid a delay of the anticipated event. As described in Section 3, a deviation in rhetorical style from the cultural norm often carries emotional meaning: directness can be perceived as aggression in indirect cultures. Hence, we are convinced that the presented CSs can be used to express emotion.

5 System Architecture

Our approaches to the automatic generation of CS are developed as part of the KRISTINA Project (Wanner et al., 2016; Meditskos et al., 2016). At the core of the aspired system, a DM component decides on the next system action. It is supported by a Knowledge Base (KB) that provides the core semantic information to a user request as RDF statement. Furthermore, the KB can be queried for further information. The DM decides whether to act independently, e.g. by requesting a confirmation of the user, or to use the statements provided by the KB in a system action. In that case, it also selects and generates a suitable CS. A language generation component transforms the semantic information it gets from the DM into sentences. This ensures the flexibility needed to generate the system output for newly devised system actions.

6 Data

In the scope of the KRISTINA project, extensive corpus recordings are being performed. The corpus encompasses over ten hours of recordings and 400 dialogues at the time of publication and the recordings are still ongoing. We train our model with conversations between German, Turkish, Polish, Spanish and Arab people. Topics include personal habits and preferences as well as medical questions, amongst others.

Current annotations cover semantic content and emotion (Sukno et al., 2016). They are being utilised and enhanced to support the automatic generation of system actions. To this end, the verbosity of a system action is derived from the number of its semantic topics. Annotators determine the directness of a

system action by assessing its intent. Where necessary, they provide the underlying semantic content.

7 Generation of Communication Styles

Variants of system action with the same semantic content but different CS must be available to the DM in order to enable adaptation. While it is possible to define a list of all system actions with all CS variations, it represents an immense amount of work. In this section, we introduce approaches to automatically generate variations of system actions with regard to their CS.

7.1 Level of Verbosity

The level of verbosity reflects how much information is given in addition to the core semantics. Answering a question with low verbosity may consist of a simple 'No'. A slight increase of verbosity might result in 'No, that is wrong', while a high level of verbosity can result in a lengthy answer such as 'No, that is wrong. This is the actual fact. Here is some further background information'.

The challenge of automatically generating verbosity is to determine relevant further information. The same KB that provides the statements of the core semantic content is used to this end. Starting with the resources of the core statements, the KB is queried for further statements that contain them. Such statements are included in the system action as additional information. By recursively repeating this process on the newly gathered statements, an arbitrary amount of additional information can be acquired. The level of verbosity chosen by the DM determines when to stop the collection of new information. This is modified by the relevance of the information: relevant information is pursued longer, while irrelevant information is disregarded.

The relevance of the acquired information is derived from the dialogues collected in the KRISTINA corpus and adjusted with each conversation the system participates in. The overall frequency of a class or property in all conversations as well as their frequency in combination with the classes and properties of the core statements is used as indication of importance. Furthermore, the relevance of an information decreases if it is present in the recent dialogue history.

By taking into consideration the user input, the core semantic content, the targeted level of verbosity and the dialogue history, which change with each dialogue turn, as well as the content of the KB and the importance rating, which also change over time, the additional content of a system action is selected based on a unique combination of input information. This results in the production diverse, ever-changing and unforeseen new system actions.

7.2 Level of Directness

The level of directness relates to the degree to which the core information is concealed. A direct way to help the user with a problem would be 'Do this.', while the indirect approach could be 'People often do this when they have that problem'. Instead of a direct question to gather missing information from the user, the system can also utilise 'I still need this information' or 'This information is missing'. Explicit and implicit confirmation strategies are a common example of different levels of directness in DM.

It is more complex to change the level of directness than that of verbosity. The semantic content of a system action needs to be changed while preserving its implications to achieve indirectness.

To generate alternative, more indirect system actions, we use predefined templates for each category of system action. For example, a request for missing information is replaced by a statement that the information is missing. The templates are chosen dynamically and filled with relevant content derived from the original system action. This approach relies on predefining all possible alternatives. We pursue two further approaches that result in a more autonomous system: supervised learning and reward functions.

The generation of indirect versions of system actions can be trained by supervised learning, using the level of directness and the core semantics, as determined by the annotators, as input data and the original semantics as target. This requires suitably annotated data. Each dialogue contribution has to be annotated with not only the actual, but also the underlying semantics. The annotators must be able to reliably determine the hidden (and possibly ambiguous) direct meaning. With our annotation of the KRISTINA corpus we make an effort to obtain suitable data. Using this approach, indirect system actions can be automatically extracted from a cor-

pus. While this improves the flexibility compared to hand-crafted templates, it does not enable the system to create new system actions autonomously. This can be achieved with reward functions.

When training with reward functions, the system tests arbitrary statements as substitute for the core statements. Those are extracted from the KB. A reward is given if the alternative version still achieves the desired goal. This way, appropriate substitutes are detected and are more likely to be generated in the future. A number of alternatives may be predefined to provide a starting point and avoid unguided exploration. For this approach, a well-defined goal for each system action is required. Furthermore, the system needs to be able to determine automatically if the goal is achieved. For questions, the goal is to get information from the user. It is achieved if the user provides the desired information. For statements, one common goal is to inform the user. The success of a statement is evaluated by requesting the user to repeat the provided information. Using reward functions is the approach with the highest amount of independence as it allows for the generation of unforeseen system actions.

8 Conclusion and Future Work

In this paper, we presented approaches to the automatic generation of new system actions that are based on changing the verbosity and directness of existing system actions. We provided exemplary applications to illustrate the potential for adaptation of those newly created system actions and proposed approaches to implement their autonomous generation.

The level of verbosity can be altered by adding semantic content retrieved from a KB to the system action. Templates can be used to provide alternative semantics for indirect system actions; machine learning approaches offer more flexibility.

In future work, we will evaluate our approaches for automatic generation of CS by confirming the soundness of the newly created system actions in the context of the dialogue. Furthermore, user studies will be conducted test the aptitude of CS to enable adaptation to the user and system emotion. Additional user studies will determine which CS is suited best for which emotion, with special consideration of the influence of the culture.

Acknowledgements

This paper is part of a project that has received funding from the European Union's Horizon 2020 research and innovation programme under grant agreement No 645012.

References

Elisabeth André, Matthias Rehm, Wolfgang Minker, and Dirk Bühler. 2004. Endowing spoken language dialogue systems with emotional intelligence. In *Affective Dialogue Systems*, pages 178–187. Springer.

Ruth Aylett and Ana Paiva. 2012. Computational modelling of culture and affect. *Emotion Review*, 4(3):253–263.

Gregor Bertrand, Florian Nothdurft, Wolfgang Minker, Harald Traue, and Steffen Walter. 2011. Adapting dialogue to user emotion-a wizard-of-oz study for adaptation strategies. *Proc. of IWSDS*, pages 285–294.

Martin Beveridge and John Fox. 2006. Automatic generation of spoken dialogue from medical plans and ontologies. *Journal of biomedical informatics*, 39(5):482–499.

Ellen Feghali. 1997. Arab cultural communication patterns. *International Journal of Intercultural Relations*, 21(3):345–378.

Milan Gnjatović and Dietmar Rösner. 2008. Adaptive dialogue management in the NIMITEK prototype system. In *Perception in Multimodal Dialogue Systems*, pages 14–25. Springer.

Rudolf Kadlec, Martin Schmid, and Jan Kleindienst. 2015. Improved deep learning baselines for ubuntu corpus dialogs. *arXiv preprint arXiv:1510.03753*.

Robert B Kaplan. 1966. Cultural thought patterns in inter-cultural education. *Language learning*, 16(1-2):1–20.

Raymond Kozlowski, Kathleen F McCoy, and K Vijay-Shanker. 2003. Generation of single-sentence paraphrases from predicate/argument structure using lexico-grammatical resources. In *Proceedings of the second international workshop on Paraphrasing-Volume 16*, pages 1–8. Association for Computational Linguistics.

Irene Langkilde and Kevin Knight. 1998. Generation that exploits corpus-based statistical knowledge. In *Proceedings of the 36th Annual Meeting of the Association for Computational Linguistics and 17th International Conference on Computational Linguistics-Volume 1*, pages 704–710. Association for Computational Linguistics.

Samuel Mascarenhas, Rui Prada, Ana Paiva, and Gert Jan Hofstede. 2013. Social importance dynamics: a model for culturally-adaptive agents. In *Intelligent virtual agents*, pages 325–338. Springer.

Georgios Meditskos, Stamatia Dasiopoulou, Louisa Pragst, Stefan Ultes, Stefanos Vrochidis, Ioannis Kompatsiaris, and Leo Wanner. 2016. Towards an ontology-driven adaptive dialogue framework. In *Proceedings of the 1st International Workshop on Multimedia Analysis and Retrieval for Multimodal Interaction*, pages 15–20. ACM.

Nobal B Niraula, Amanda Stent, Hyuckchul Jung, Giuseppe Di Fabbrizio, I Dan Melamed, and Vasile Rus. 2014. Forms2dialog: Automatic dialog generation for web tasks. In *Spoken Language Technology Workshop (SLT), 2014 IEEE*, pages 608–613. IEEE.

Johannes Pittermann and Angela Pittermann. 2007. A data-oriented approach to integrate emotions in adaptive dialogue management. In *Proceedings of the 12th international conference on Intelligent user interfaces*, pages 270–273. ACM.

Louisa Pragst. 2015. Multimodal adaptive dialogue management in OwlSpeak.

Verena Rieser and Oliver Lemon. 2011. *Reinforcement learning for adaptive dialogue systems: a data-driven methodology for dialogue management and natural language generation*. Springer Science & Business Media.

Federico Sukno, Mónica Domínguez, Adria Ruiz, Dominik Schiller, Florian Lingenfelser, Louisa Pragst, Eleni Kamateri, and Stefanos Vrochidis. 2016. A multimodal annotation schema for non-verbal affective analysis in the health-care domain. In *Proceedings of the 1st International Workshop on Multimedia Analysis and Retrieval for Multimodal Interaction*, pages 9–14. ACM.

Stefan Ultes and Wolfgang Minker. 2014. Managing adaptive spoken dialogue for intelligent environments. *Journal of Ambient Intelligence and Smart Environments*, 6(5):523–539.

Leo Wanner, Josep Blat, Stamatia Dasiopoulou, Mónica Domínguez, Gerard Llorach, Simon Mille, Federico Sukno, Eleni Kamateri, Ioannis Kompatsiaris, Stefanos Vrochidis, et al. 2016. Towards a multimedia knowledge-based agent with social competence and human interaction capabilities. In *Proceedings of the 1st International Workshop on Multimedia Analysis and Retrieval for Multimodal Interaction*, pages 21–26. ACM.

Ke Zhai and Jason D Williams. 2014. Discovering latent structure in task-oriented dialogues. In *ACL (1)*, pages 36–46.

Mining Knowledge in Storytelling Systems for Narrative Generation

Eugenio Concepción and **Pablo Gervás** and **Gonzalo Méndez**
Facultad de Informática
Instituto de Tecnología del Conocimiento
Universidad Complutense de Madrid
`{econcepc,pgervas,gmendez}@ucm.es`

Abstract

Storytelling systems are computational systems designed to tell stories. Every story generation system defines its specific knowledge representation for supporting the storytelling process. Thus, there is a shared need amongst all the systems: the knowledge must be expressed unambiguously to avoid inconsistencies. However, when trying to make a comparative assessment between the storytelling systems, there is not a common way for expressing this knowledge. That is when a form of expression that covers the different aspects of the knowledge representations becomes necessary. A suitable solution is the use of a Controlled Natural Language (CNL) which is a good half-way point between natural and formal languages. A CNL can be used as a common medium of expression for this heterogeneous set of systems. This paper proposes the use of Controlled Natural Language for expressing every storytelling system knowledge as a collection of natural language sentences. In this respect, an initial grammar for a CNL is proposed, focusing on certain aspects of this knowledge.

1 Introduction

Natural language is the most basic form of knowledge representation for the humans, because it allows communication and knowledge transmission. Natural languages provide an unbeatable expressivity for concept modelling and structuring. However, for the same reasons they are substantially complex for automatic processing.

A Controlled Natural Language (CNL) is an engineered subset of natural languages whose grammar and vocabulary have been restricted in a systematic way in order to reduce both ambiguity and complexity of full natural languages (Schwitter, 2010). CNL can be considered as a tradeoff between the expressivity of the natural languages, and the need for the orthogonality of a formal representation that can be handled by a computer.

Story generation systems are a form of expression for computational creativity. According to (Gervás, 2012), a story generator algorithm (SGA) refers to a computational procedure resulting in an artefact that can be considered a story. The term story generation system can be considered as a synonym of storytelling systems, that is, a computational system designed to tell stories.

Story generation system are faced with a significant challenge of acquiring knowledge resources in the particular representation formats that they use. They face a inherent difficulty when using formal languages in the detachment between the formulation of the needs in the real world and its representation in a formal construction.

In this context, the use of a CNL would provide the means for a quicker development of required resources in a format easier to write for human experts. So, the use of a CNL for codifying resources for storytelling systems might provide some advantage. If authors of storytelling systems were to develop the initial version of their resources in a commonly agreed CNL, and then develop the appropriate automated transformations to generate knowledge in their own preferred format, the same resources writ-

Proceedings of the INLG 2016 Workshop on Computational Creativity and Natural Language Generation, pages 41–50,
Edinburgh, September 2016. ©2016 Association for Computational Linguistics

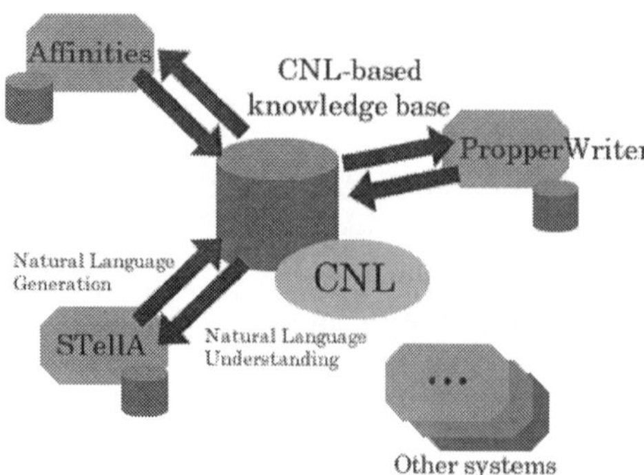

Figure 1: Architecture of the shared CNL-based knowledge base system.

ten in CNL might be of use to researchers developing different storytelling systems. Some previous studies on this matter can be found in (Schwitter, 2010), (Kuhn, 2009), (Power et al., 2009), (Davis et al., 2009), (Fuchs et al., 2008), and (Funk et al., 2007).

Particularly, the use of a CNL for knowledge representation has been documented previously (Kuhn, 2009), and (Barzdins, 2014). In both cases, these precedent works are quite convenient with respect to information extraction of and reasoning with the content of texts.

This paper proposes a model of a Controlled Natural Language understood as a means for mining knowledge from existing storytelling systems.

This process is part of a wider project which aims at the development of a collaborative environment involving several story generation systems.

The purpose of this environment is to establish a co-creation architectural model which allows the involved systems to take advantage of a shared knowledge base and use it for enhancing the quality of the generated texts. The architecture of this system is schematically depicted in the Figure 1. In the current stage of the model, the NLG step is used for translating the system-specific formalisms into the common CNL statements. In the final model, there will be an additional NLG step when generating the refined story.

The thrust of this approach is the use of a CNL as a shared representation for the various knowledge models of the different story generation sys-

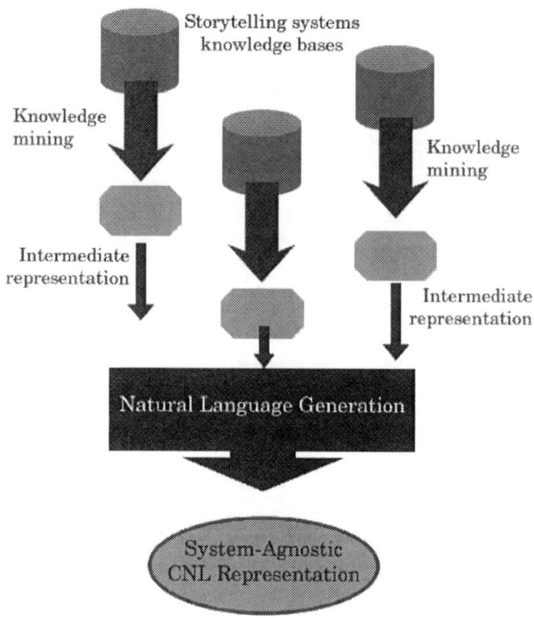

Figure 2: Knowledge Mining process applied to Natural Language Generation.

tems. Ideally, every custom representation should be translated into the common CNL for being subsequently employed. In this way, the story generation process will result in a build-up of contributions from different systems. For example, one of the depicted systems, labeled as *Affinities* (Méndez et al., 2016), is specialized in characters interactions and affinities, but it lacks in a deeper enhancement of the narrative discourse, that can be compensated by STellA (León and Gervás, 2011).

The drafted architecture aims at several objectives. Firstly, it intends to establish a collaborative model that allows the free exchange of knowledge between the different storytelling systems in order to develop an iterative improvement process of literary creation. Beside this objective, it promotes the development of a knowledge representation model for creating a common, system-agnostic knowledge base that can be feed in the future with the outcomes of new storytelling systems, without the need to adapt their knowledge representation models.

The scope of this paper relates only to the Natural Language Generation step, as depicted in the Figure 2.

2 Related Work

2.1 Natural Language Generation

The process of Natural Language Generation has been clearly defined (Reiter et al., 2000), as well as its six distinctive tasks:

- Content Determination: in which the generation system makes a decision concerning the information that will be taken into account for generating the text.

- Discourse Planning: this task involves decisions about how the text should be globally articulated.

- Lexicalisation: in which the generation system makes a choice of the particular words and phrases it considers suitable to convey the semantics of the selected information, in the given natural language and its context.

- Aggregation: this task involves decisions concerning the composition of the generated sentences to form a natural discourse.

- Referring Expression Generation: this task involves the determination of the properties of a given linguistic element, which to be used when the element is mentioned again.

- Surface Realisation: the last task that reviews the text for checking that it presents syntactically, morphologically and orthographically correct sentences in the corresponding natural language.

Many different architectures have been proposed for NLG systems, reflecting the range of different applications and its purposes. Basically, there are two main models of the NLG process: the Abstract Generation System (Bateman, 1997) and the Abstract Referential Model, an outcome of the Reference Architecture for Generation Systems (RAGS) (Cahill et al., 2000) which is aiming at standards for NLG architecture.

2.2 Knowledge Representation in Storytelling Systems

From an historical perspective, formal languages have been the most common way of knowledge representation. The reason for using formal languages is simplicity; they have a well-defined syntax, an unambiguous semantics and they are very convenient for automated reasoning. Particularly, in the field of automatic story generation, there is an abundance of examples of this kind.

TALE-SPIN (Meehan, 1977a) was one of the earlier story generators. It was a problem solver, top-down and goal-directed story generation engine. TALE-SPIN generated stories about the inhabitants of a forest taking a collection of characters with their corresponding objectives as inputs. TALE-SPIN found a solution for those characters goals, and wrote up a story narrating the steps performed for achieving those goals.

TALE-SPIN knowledge representation relied on Conceptual Dependency Theory (Schank and Abelson, 1975). It used a set of primitives for representing the problem domain. All its knowledge was expressed as a formal language.

Minstrel (Turner, 1993) was a story generation system that told stories about King Arthur and his Knights of the Round Table. Each story was focused on a moral, which also provided the seed for developing the story.

The knowledge representation in Minstrel used an extension of a Lisp library called Rhapsody. Rhapsody was a tools package for AI program development that provided the user with ways to declare and manipulate simple frame-style representations, and a number of tools for building programs that use them.

Mexica (Perez y Perez, 1999) was developed as a computer model whose purpose was studying the creative process. It generated short stories about the early inhabitants of Mexico. Mexica was a pioneer in that it took into account emotional links and tensions between the characters as a means for driving and evaluating ongoing stories.

Mexica used several knowledge structures for supporting its storytelling model: An actions library, a collection of stories for inspiring the new ones, and a group of characters and locations. The generation process also took several steps, in which data were progressively transformed.

Mexica knowledge management involves several concerns in order to provide a high-quality outcome, in terms of literary production. Its knowledge base included several types of structures for representing things like characters relationships, actions, emotional links, and a literary base composed of previously generated stories.

Brutus (Bringsjord and Ferrucci, 2000) was a system that generated short stories using betrayal as leitmotiv. It had a rich logical model for representing betrayal. This feature allowed it to generate complex stories. A very innovative aspect of Brutus was that it considered the existing body of knowledge about literature and grammar for generating stories.

Brutus structured its knowledge in several layers, including a grammar specific part. So, the process of converting the plot into the final output was carried out by the application of a hierarchy of grammars: story grammars, paragraph grammars and sentence grammars. This hierarchical procedure led to define every story as a sequence of paragraphs which in turn were sequences of sentences.

MAKEBELIEVE (Liu and Singh, 2002) was a short fictional story generation system that used common sense knowledge to generate stories. The user provided a story about a character as initial seed, and then MAKEBELIEVE attempted to continue that story by inferring possible sequences of events that might happen to that character. The system used common sense knowledge about causality and how the world works, mined from the Open Mind Common Sense knowledge base (Singh et al., 2002).

STellA (Story Telling Algorithm) (León and Gervás, 2014) is a story generation system that controls and chooses states in a non-deterministically generated space of partial stories until it finds a satisfactory simulation of events that is rendered as a story.

STellA uses a custom representation for the knowledge it needs. It manages several different structures, including a matrix representation of the world in which characters live, and a set of rules for evaluating the range of results associated to the actions.

2.3 Use of CNLs in Storytelling Systems

There is not a long record of application of CNLs in the context of storytelling.

Inform (Reed, 2010) was a toolset for creating interactive fiction. As from version 7, Inform provided a domain-specific language for defining the primary aspects of an interactive fiction like the world setting, the character features, and the story flow. The provided domain-specific language used a CNL, similar to Attempto Controlled English (Fuchs et al., 1998).

The StoryBricks (Campbell, 2011) framework was an interactive story design system. It provided a graphical editing language based on Scratch (Resnick et al., 2009) that allowed users to edit both the characters features and the logic that drove their behaviour in the game. By means of special components named story bricks, users could define the world in which characters live, define their emotions, and supply them with items. Story bricks were blocks containing words to create sentences in natural language when placed together. They served to define rules that apply under certain conditions during the development of the story in the game.

In the extended ATTAC-L version (Broeckhoven et al., 2015), authors introduced a model which combined the use of a graphical Domain Specific Modeling Language (DSML) for modelling serious games narrative, ATTAC-L (Broeckhoven and Troyer, 2013), with a CNL to open the use of the DSML to a broader range of users, for which they selected Attempto Controlled English (Fuchs et al., 1998). It allows describing things in logical terms, predicates, formulas, and quantification statements. All its sentences are built by means of two word classes: function words (determiners, quantifiers, negation words, etc.) and content words (nouns, verbs, adverbs and prepositions). The main advantage is that Attempto Controlled English defines a strict and finite set of unambiguous constructions and interpretation rules.

3 Conceptual Basis

Towards the definition of a shared representation, we will review previously the main aspects of the knowledge involved in storytelling systems.

Narrative has different aspects in terms of representation (Gervás and León, 2014), each of which has a different natural structure. Every story generation system focuses in a subset of these aspects and holds them by means of a certain set of data structures that represents the system knowledge. For example, Brutus (Bringsjord and Ferrucci, 2000) and

Minstrel (Turner, 1993) emphasised the thematic aspect of the narrative, that is the central topic a text treats. Brutus main theme was betrayal, while every Minstrel story started on a moral that was used as the initial seed.

Still on this subject, another relevant conclusion mentioned by (Gervás and León, 2014) is that the same information may be represented through different data structures without affecting its essence, or a data structure can be extended for representing additional types of information. For example, Brutus (Bringsjord and Ferrucci, 2000) used a specific representation for representing the betrayal. Brutus was developed using a logic-programming system called FLEX, which is based on the programming language Prolog. Its knowledge about betrayal was modelled by a set of statements in FLEX, called *frames*. Every frame formalized the essential characteristics of betrayal: the betrayer, the betrayed, the locations, the actions involved, etc. Mexica (Perez y Perez, 1999) used a wider representation of the relationships between the characters, not specifically focused on betrayal. Relations in Mexica are of two types: emotional links and tensions. Emotional links represent affective reactions between characters. They are defined in terms of three attributes: type (love or friendship), valence (positive or negative) and intensity. Tensions represent if there is a conflict between two characters. It is defined by a type (of conflict) and a state (on or off).

In both examples the same narrative aspect is represented differently in every system, but it can be conceptually identified as a shared concern.

3.1 Dimensions of the narrative

For the purpose of this paper, we are considering a previous work of (Gervás and León, 2014), who analysed the most relevant classifications of the story generation systems according to the knowledge they managed, and proposed their own list of suitable dimensions obtained from the different aspects of a narrative:

- The discourse sequence aspect: a sequential discourse of conceptually conveyed items.

- The simulation aspect: a representation of the activity of agents in terms of actions, interactions, mental states, and movement between locations.

- The causal aspect: a structured representation of causal relations between elements in the story.

- The intentional aspect: a representation of the motivations of agents.

- The thematic aspect: a representation of the theme of parts of the story.

- The emotional aspect: a representation of the emotions involved in or produced by the story.

- The authorial aspect: a representation of the intentions of the author.

- The narrative structure aspect: representations of the story in terms of narratological concepts of story structure.

3.2 Considerations for grammar definition

In addition to these semantic aspects, the proposed CNL grammar definition should meet the common requirements expressed by (Kuhn, 2010):

- Concreteness: CNL grammars should be fully formalized and interpretable by computers.

- Declarativeness: CNL grammars should not depend on a concrete algorithm or implementation.

- Lookahead Features: CNL grammars should allow for the retrieval of possible next tokens for a partial text.

- Anaphoric References: CNL grammars should allow for the denition of nonlocal structures like anaphoric references.

- Implementability: CNL grammars should be easy to implement in different programming languages.

- Expressivity: CNL grammars should be sufficiently expressive to express CNLs.

One of the major challenges that faces the target representation is to provide a unambiguous formalism while keeping Natural Language expressiveness.

4 A proposed representation for the narrative dimension

The dimension considered firstly in the CNL grammar is the narrative aspect. It focuses on identifying the underlying structure of the narrative, understood as the framework that supports the inner consistency of the story. From a procedural point of view, the narrative aspect defines the actions performed in order to enhance this skeleton, providing a progressively enriched narrative as a result. This dimension can be traced in the knowledge representation of several of the referred systems (Meehan, 1977b; Dehn, 1981; Turner, 1993; Perez y Perez, 1999; León and Gervás, 2014)

As noted by (Gervás and León, 2014), a different fundamental aspect of narrative is the fact that it can be analyzed in terms of recurring structures that articulate its main ingredients into abstractions that allow its description at a higher level than simple enumerations of events. Along this same line, Propp work (Propp, 1968) is an effort for systematizing the representation of this aspect.

Lang works provided a very interesting step forward to this matter (Lang, 1999) by developing a declarative model for simple narratives. This model described stories in terms of a sequence of events, trying to provide a combined response to the two traditional approaches: declarative and procedural. In the declarative approach the generated text fits a structure that has been defined before (Rumelhart, 1975). By contrast, in the procedural approach, the text was modelled according to a creation process that emulated human authors (Lebowitz, 1985; Turner, 1993).

4.1 Story structure

The proposed structure for representing stories is conceptually based on previous work (Lang, 1999), in the sense of a story is composed by a setting and an episode list, which both have temporal intervals associated with them.

Every episode can be expressed as a N-tuple composed of four elements:

- An initiating event

- An emotional response on the part of the protagonist

- An action response on the part of the protagonist

- An outcome or state description which holds at the conclusion of the episode

4.2 Vocabulary definition

The vocabulary provides the terms for sustaining the conceptual model of every specific dimension. Each dimension can be considered as a domain itself, understood as a unit composed by a cohesive set of interconnected concepts. These concepts are provided by a collection of domain terms and their relations. So, they are the building units for expressing the knowledge relevant for the considered dimensions. In order to formalize this structure, the vocabulary is defined as follows:

- A *term* designates a significant knowledge entity that can be represented by a common noun or a noun phrase.

- A *name* designates unambiguously a significant entity that represents a single thing. It is typically a proper name, referring a character, a place, an object, etc.

- A *verb* designates a relationship, situation, or action involving one or more terms or names. The verbs are both the richest and the most complex elements of the vocabulary. A verb can be expressed in an active or a passive form. Verbs can also be qualified by modal verbs, so they can communicate probability, ability, permission, obligation and advice.

- An *adverbial* serves for expressing the circumstances involving the action defined by the verb. It is an optional part of the sentence.

4.3 Grammar definition

The expression *Subject + Verb* defines an attribution or a state related to the Subject, that is a placeholder for a Term or a Name.

The combination *Subject + Verb + Object* defines a semantic relationship and has two placeholders filled by Terms/Names. The particular case of the verb to be must be considered as a typical expression for building descriptions.

The combination *Subject* + *Verb* + *[Adverbial]* + *Object* defines an action performed over an object. The action defined by the verb can be better put into context by means of adverbials. These can be used for expressing the circumstances in which action takes place.

Sentences can be combined in order to create compound sentences or subordinate clauses.

The sentence will be expressed in a declarative manner. For example, the following statement shows a complete case:

The main character finds accidentally a clue that allows him to finish his research.

The CNL grammar defines a collection of syntax rules and constrains for representing the knowledge as statements. It presupposes the existence of a vocabulary because it addresses the *terms* and *verbs* defined in the vocabulary. The general structure of every statement is composed of four parts: the initiating event, an optional part that expresses a change in the subject emotions, another optional part that expresses the actions taken by the subject, and a ending sentence that expresses the outcome.

So far, we have presented the general pattern of the grammar. It is a set of rules which allow going from a simple to a reasonably complex structure. This last point can be reached by means of connectives. The noun phrases can also be combined and qualified using different quantifications and prepositional phrases, but always with the certainty that it will produce sentences that are grammatically correct.

5 A proposed representation for the simulation dimension

Another relevant aspect of narrative is the representation of characters, their behaviour, and the expression of their mental state, their relations with one another, their motivations, and their beliefs. The simulation aspect has been frequently highlighted as the leitmotiv for the representation of narratives in some approaches to story generation (Lebowitz, 1985; Bringsjord and Ferrucci, 2000). Such approaches usually focus on representing characters and rules that may govern their behaviour and interaction.

5.1 Modelling the affinity

The simulation aspect refers to the characterization of the persona in terms of the interaction between each other. That is, this aspect covers a wide scope that ranges from the definition of characters attributes and traits, to the delimitation of their affinities. Naturally, this also relates to the way in which the characters interact with each other and the actions they perform motivated by the result of such interactions. The affinity aspect have been studied by several authors and systems (Imbert and De Antonio, 2005; Si et al., 2006; Méndez et al., 2016). The present work is related to the system developed by (Méndez et al., 2016). Usually, the authors apply an affinity factor for modelling the way in which social interaction affects the behaviour of the characters with each other. In other cases, affinity is affected by other factors, such as social obligations and characters goals. An additional aspect of affinity to keep in mind is that it is not symmetrical. Given two characters, their mutual affinity is likely to be dissimilar.

There are several possible ways for expressing the affinity between two characters. A first option is the use of a collection of symbolic values that allow reasoning about them and the ongoing simulation, but that difficult the operation. On the other hand, the use of numeric values makes easier operating with them, but hinders understanding the evolution of the simulation.

With a view to representing the affinity in terms of Natural Language, the simpler choice is to use a collection of adjectives that represent a range of numeric values.

In the referred model (Méndez et al., 2016), authors have modelled additionally four levels of affinity according to four different kinds of affinity: *foe* (no affinity), *indifferent* (slight affinity), *friend* (medium affinity) and *mate* (high affinity). These values can be suitable for expressing it in a first approach.

5.2 Vocabulary definition

As stated previously, the vocabulary provides the terms for defining the model of the corresponding dimension. In the domain of the simulation, the vocabulary is defined as follows:

- A *term* designates a significant knowledge entity that can be represented by a common noun or a noun phrase. It is exactly as defined in the context of narrative structure.

- A *name* designates unambiguously a significant entity that represents a single thing. It is exactly the same entity as in the case of the narrative structure.

- A *verb* states a feature, a trait, or an action involving one or more terms or names. The verb in the simulation aspect provides basically a definition or an action performed by a character

5.3 Grammar definition

The simulation aspect is defined in terms of characters' traits and interactions. These special features need a specific way of being represented.

In this regard, the CNL created for expressing all these dimensions will contain basically sentences for describing traits and attributing features. It will also be a language for describing actions and interaction. So, the grammar for formalizing it is composed of expressions of the following kind: *Subject + Verb + Attribute* or: *Subject + Verb + Object*.

In the first case, the expression reflects the definition of a trait or a feature. The *attribute* will be represented by means of a *term*. The *verb* will typically be the *to be* and *to have*.

In the second case, the verb expresses an action. The character, that is the subject, performs some action that affects something or someone. So, the *object* can be either a *term* or a *name*.

This last type of expression can also be used for defining the affinity between characters, so there will be sentences like: *John is a friend of Mary.*

6 Conclusions and future work

This paper proposed the application of a CNL for eliciting and exchanging knowledge between story generation systems as a means of collaborative generation of stories. It also discusses a model for generating this CNL automatically from different knowledge representation formalisms. As explained above, there have been precedents of the use of CNL in the interactive storytelling domain with satisfactory results.

The aim of the proposed representation is to help bridging the variety of knowledge representation in a simple and formal way. The proposed syntax has been defined by a formal grammar but the resulting expressions keep a human-friendly nature.

In this paper, the developed work is centred on two dimensions of the knowledge: the story structure dimension and the simulation dimension. This is just one part of the needed multi-aspectual representation. As mentioned above, there are some other dimensions that must be addressed in future versions of the CNL: the authorial aspect, the emotional aspect, the intentional aspect and the theme aspect.

The future work will be focused on completing the set of the grammar generation rules for expressing these remaining aspects of knowledge involved in storytelling. This work will provide a completely expressive representation that hold co–creation between storytelling systems.

Benchmarking this work can really be complex, and will probably involve a shared effort with other research groups. So, we are working on proposing a shared task in which to compare the quality of stories generated by different systems using the same initial knowledge base. Collaborators will be provided with a grammar definition of a CNL that represents the narrative aspects mentioned in the previous section, along with a set of initial situations written using this grammar from which to generate different stories using the same CNL. They will be required to use as much information as possible in order to generate rich stories that cover one or more of the previously described narrative aspects. These stories must be expressed in the same CNL used to describe the initial situation so that, hypothetically, the output of a system might feed another system in order to provide more details about some of the aspects that may have been left uncovered by previous generators, following a co–creation process where a system can strengthen the weaknesses of another. The outcome of this collaborative process is expected to provide the means to develop an enhanced story creation model.

Aknowledgements

This work was partially supported by the projects WHIM (611560) and ConCreTe (611733), funded by the European Commission under FP7, the ICT theme, and the Future Emerging Technologies (FET) program.

References

Guntis Barzdins. 2014. Framenet cnl: A knowledge representation and information extraction language. In *International Workshop on Controlled Natural Language*, pages 90–101. Springer.

John A Bateman. 1997. Enabling technology for multilingual natural language generation: the kpml development environment. *Natural Language Engineering*, 3(01):15–55.

Selmer Bringsjord and David A Ferrucci. 2000. Artificial intelligence and literary creativity: Inside the mind of brutus, a storytelling machine. *Computational Linguistics*, 26(4).

Frederik Van Broeckhoven and Olga De Troyer. 2013. Attac-l: A modeling language for educational virtual scenarios in the context of preventing cyber bullying. In *2nd International Conference on Serious Games and Applications for Health*, pages 1–8. IEEE, May.

Frederik Van Broeckhoven, Joachim Vlieghe, and Olga De Troyer. 2015. Using a controlled natural language for specifying the narratives of serious games. In *8th International Conference on Interactive Digital Storytelling, ICIDS 2015*, pages 142–153.

Lynne J Cahill, Christy Doran, Roger Evans, Rodger Kibble, Chris Mellish, Daniel S Paiva, Mike Reape, Donia Scott, and Neil Tipper. 2000. Enabling resource sharing in language generation: an abstract reference architecture. In *LREC*. Citeseer.

MacGregor Campbell. 2011. A new way to play: Make your own games. *New Scientist*, 211(2829):21.

Brian Davis, Pradeep Varma, Siegfried Handschuh, Laura Dragan, and Hamish Cunningham. 2009. Controlled natural language for semantic annotation. In *The Semantic Web: Research and Applications*, pages 816–820. Springer.

Natlie Dehn. 1981. Story generation after tale-spin. In *IJCAI*, volume 81, pages 16–18.

Norbert E Fuchs, Uta Schwertel, and Rolf Schwitter. 1998. Attempto controlled englishnot just another logic specification language. In *Logic-based program synthesis and transformation*, pages 1–20. Springer.

Norbert E Fuchs, Kaarel Kaljurand, and Tobias Kuhn. 2008. Attempto controlled english for knowledge representation. In *Reasoning Web*, pages 104–124. Springer.

Adam Funk, Valentin Tablan, Kalina Bontcheva, Hamish Cunningham, Brian Davis, and Siegfried Handschuh. 2007. *Clone: Controlled language for ontology editing*. Springer.

P. Gervás and C. León. 2014. The need for multiaspectual representation of narratives in modelling their creative process. In *5th Workshop on Computational Models of Narrative*, OASIcs-OpenAccess Series in Informatics.

P. Gervás. 2012. Story generator algorithms. In *The Living Handbook of Narratology*. Hamburg University Press.

Ricardo Imbert and Angélica De Antonio. 2005. An emotional architecture for virtual characters. In *Virtual Storytelling. Using Virtual Reality Technologies for Storytelling*, pages 63–72. Springer.

Tobias Kuhn. 2009. *Controlled English for knowledge representation*. Ph.D. thesis, Faculty of Economics, Business Administration and Information Technology of the University of Zurich.

Tobias Kuhn. 2010. Codeco: A practical notation for controlled english grammars in predictive editors. In *Controlled Natural Language*, pages 95–114. Springer.

Raymond Lang. 1999. A declarative model for simple narratives. In *Proceedings of the AAAI fall symposium on narrative intelligence*, pages 134–141.

Michael Lebowitz. 1985. Storytelling and generalization. In *Seventh Annual Conference of the Cognitive Science Society*, pages 100–109.

Carlos León and Pablo Gervás. 2011. A top-down design methodology based on causality and chronology for developing assisted story generation systems. In *Proceedings of the 8th ACM conference on Creativity and cognition*, pages 363–364. ACM.

Carlos León and Pablo Gervás. 2014. Creativity in story generation from the ground up: Nondeterministic simulation driven by narrative. In *5th International Conference on Computational Creativity, ICCC*.

Hugo Liu and Push Singh. 2002. Makebelieve: Using commonsense knowledge to generate stories. In Rina Dechter and Richard S. Sutton, editors, *AAAI/IAAI*, pages 957–958. AAAI Press / The MIT Press.

James R. Meehan. 1977a. Tale-spin, an interactive program that writes stories. In *In Proceedings of the Fifth International Joint Conference on Artificial Intelligence*, pages 91–98.

James R Meehan. 1977b. Tale-spin, an interactive program that writes stories. In *IJCAI*, volume 77, pages 91–98.

Gonzalo Méndez, Pablo Gervás, and Carlos León. 2016. On the use of character affinities for story plot generation. In *Knowledge, Information and Creativity Support Systems*, pages 211–225. Springer.

R. Perez y Perez. 1999. *MEXICA: A Computer Model of Creativity in Writing*. Ph.D. thesis, The University of Sussex.

Richard Power, Robert Stevens, Donia Scott, and Alan Rector. 2009. Editing owl through generated cnl.

Vladimir Propp. 1968. Morphology of the folk tale. 1928.

A. Reed. 2010. *Creating Interactive Fiction with Inform 7*. Cengage Learning.

Ehud Reiter, Robert Dale, and Zhiwei Feng. 2000. *Building natural language generation systems*, volume 33. MIT Press.

Mitchel Resnick, John Maloney, Andrés Monroy-Hernández, Natalie Rusk, Evelyn Eastmond, Karen Brennan, Amon Millner, Eric Rosenbaum, Jay Silver, Brian Silverman, and Yasmin Kafai. 2009. Scratch: Programming for all. *Commun. ACM*, 52(11):60–67, November.

David E Rumelhart. 1975. Notes on a schema for stories. *Representation and understanding: Studies in cognitive science*, 211(236):45.

Roger C. Schank and Robert P. Abelson. 1975. Scripts, plans, and knowledge. In *Proceedings of the 4th International Joint Conference on Artificial Intelligence - Volume 1*, IJCAI'75, pages 151–157, San Francisco, CA, USA. Morgan Kaufmann Publishers Inc.

Rolf Schwitter. 2010. Controlled natural languages for knowledge representation. In *Proceedings of the 23rd International Conference on Computational Linguistics: Posters*, COLING '10, pages 1113–1121, Stroudsburg, PA, USA. Association for Computational Linguistics.

Mei Si, Stacy C Marsella, and David V Pynadath. 2006. Thespian: Modeling socially normative behavior in a decision-theoretic framework. In *Intelligent Virtual Agents*, pages 369–382. Springer.

P. Singh, T. Lin, E. T. Mueller, G. Lim, T. Perkins, and W. L. Zhu. 2002. Open mind common sense: Knowledge acquisition from the general public. In *On the move to meaningful internet systems 2002: Coopis, DOA and Odbase*, pages 1223–1237. Springer.

Scott R. Turner. 1993. *Minstrel: A Computer Model of Creativity and Storytelling*. Ph.D. thesis, University of California at Los Angeles, Los Angeles, CA, USA. UMI Order no. GAX93-19933.

Process Based Evaluation of Computer Generated Poetry

Stephen McGregor and **Matthew Purver** and **Geraint Wiggins**
Queen Mary University of London
School of Electronic Engineering and Computer Science
s.e.mcgregor@qmul.ac.uk   m.purver@qmul.ac.uk
geraint.wiggins@qmul.ac.uk

Abstract

This paper presents and evaluates a novel system for computer generated poetry. Framed within contemporary theoretical trends in the evaluation of computational creativity, we investigate how evidence of generative process influences readers' opinions of computer generated textual output. In addition to a technical description of our system, we present results from a study asking respondents to evaluate short computer generated poems prefaced with different types of descriptions, in some cases objectively presenting the poem as the product of a statistical analysis of corpora and in some cases subjectively presenting the computer as a self-aware agent.

1 Introduction

The trope of the poet as inscrutable genius figures large in our collective cultural appreciation of poetry. Coleridge emerging from a drunken stupor with the lines to "Kubla Kahn" fully formed in his mind, Blake hallucinating trees full of angels, the drunken, stoned verse of Rimbaud and Verlaine, the psychic divinations of Breton and Soupault: regardless of the legitimacy of these legends, we as readers are seduced by the idea of the poet as a transmitter of the ineffable, tapped into an mental space inaccessible and unknowable to most of us.

Of course when it comes to computers, we are not willing to give them this kind of credit, nor should we be. When we encounter a machine that produces exemplary poetry, we suspect there might be an element of human interference lurking in the mechanism. Such output, without any explanation of the generative procedure employed by the system, including its engagement with a corpus of relevant extant cultural artefacts, is subject to suspicions of pastiche or even plagiarism. The burden of creative justification is on the system itself: it is reasonable to expect a creative computational agent to justify its output in terms of the way in which it was generated, and in particular to demonstrate the way in which its procedures can be ostensibly construed as instances of autonomous engagement with an existing *inspiring set* (Ritchie, 2012). The judgment of discerning observers of computational output will ultimately be influenced by the effectiveness of this presentation of process.

In this study, we systematically test the difference between how human readers react to poems generated by computers when the computational process is, on the one hand, framed as a procedure of statistical analysis, and, on the other hand, as a creative endeavour undertaken by an autonomous and ostensibly self-aware agent. In both cases, we are exploring the ways in which humans react to creative artefacts which have been openly generated by computers; in this work, we are not concerned with exploring the ability of human observers to distinguish between work created by other humans versus output covertly generated by computational processes. The appreciation of creative work is always a moving target, in that popular opinions of what qualifies as innovation is perpetually evolving, and our stance is that public consideration of art is moving towards a point where the idea of creative machines is becoming increasingly palatable. In this regard in particular, we feel that poetry generated by processes transparently

Proceedings of the INLG 2016 Workshop on Computational Creativity and Natural Language Generation, pages 51–60,
Edinburgh, September 2016. ©2016 Association for Computational Linguistics

grounded in the machine learning paradigm will be judged favourably.

In this paper, we'll begin with a overview of computational creativity, focusing in particular on ideas about the evaluation of not only creative artefacts but also creative processes. The nature of our study is motivated by an examination of some specific examples of computational poetry generating systems. In Section 3, we'll outline the technical details of a novel system for generating short, simple poems, grounded in statistical analyses of large sets of textual data. In Section 4, we'll present a study collecting evaluations of our systems output influenced by different ways of presenting the computational process behind the generation of the output. In our final analysis, we will discover that the procedural presentation does not, in fact, influence the ratings returned by readers, at least to a statistically significant degree, and at least for the type of highly autonomous output produced by the system which we'll describe here.

2 Computers, Creativity, and Poetry

This paper is in particular concerned with the evaluation of computer generated poetry. With this in mind, however, an overview of recent and ongoing general trends in the field of computational creativity seems an appropriate starting point. In particular here we're concerned with presenting some thoughts on the question of the evaluation of creative work undertaken by computational agents, and in particular the issue of the assessment of computational process as a critical element in this kind of evaluation.

2.1 Evaluating Computational Creativity

While the concept of the Turing Test – the behaviouralist assessment of a symbol manipulating system sheerly on the basis of its output – has captured the popular imagination, the field of Computational Creativity has probably since its inception been concerned not only with the evaluation of artefacts produced by machines but also with the perception of the machine itself as a producer. (Boden, 1990), for instance, is generally concerned with the importance of self-evaluation in the creative process, and in particular considers the way in which the "computer's performance" (p. 159) contributes

to the perception of aesthetic value in the case of computer generated art. More recently, (Colton and Wiggins, 2012) have advocated "assessing the behaviour of software via process rather than product" (p. 24), by way of creative systems *"framing* their creative acts with information that adds value" (p. 25, emphasis in original).

The work presented here has been undertaken very much in this spirit of offering the computational process behind the generation of our system's output as an element of the artefact itself. In fact, in line with (Jordanous, 2015), we feel that much of what counts as creativity exists not merely within the creative agent, but also in the dynamic between agent, audience, and environment. In the specific case of the new system for poetry generation which will be described throughout Section 3, the computational agent engages with the world through a set of statistical analyses with large scale, highly public corpora, spanning the canonical and the encyclopedic. Our hope is that, on multiple levels, this kind of engagement with data-in-the-world or, alternatively, world-as-data offers a perspective on an agent which is situated in an accessible and even familiar environment.

Notably, this idea of statistical analysis as environmental grounding has likewise been adopted by the field of cognitive science, where, for instance, (Barsalou, 2008) has proposed the integration of statistical information about words and linguistic structures as part of a model of cognition as grounded in dynamic environmental processes. The upshot of this kind of theory is that there is some hope of understanding the seam between words and ideas in terms of the data that is available in large scale corpora, that cultural level of linguistic phenomena between the evolutionary and the developmental which has been described by (Smith et al., 2003) as *glossogenetic*. For this reason, we think that the machine learning paradigm in particular, which takes as its basis corpora on the comprehensive scale of large cultural repositories such as an exhaustive encyclopedia or a literary canon, is an appropriate setting for exploring computer generated poetry as a creative process.

2.2 Computer Generated Poetry

The prevalent trend in computer generated poetry to date has involved a combination of rule-based manipulations of symbols and clever heuristic data mining designed to populate templates affording varying degrees of freedom. The WASP system (Gervás, 2000), for instance, uses a battery of "judges" to evaluate an unfolding "draft" of a poem along a series of criteria such as rhyme, scansion, line length, and so forth. The resulting poem is a product of the interaction of these various weighted constraints, coupled with n-gram driven text generation based on an analysis of a corpus of canonical Spanish poetry. Similarly, PoeTryMe (Oliveira, 2012) employs a network of information processing nodes that interact to generate grammatical, metrical verse.

Moving into a more statistical mode of production, (Toivanen et al., 2012) describe a poetry generating system which discovers semantic relationships based on word co-occurrence statistics in a large scale corpus. In addition to this statistical technique for modelling semantics, this system imposes additional syntactic and phonological constraints on its output, and in this regard is comparable with the system described in this paper. Also within the general family of statistical, corpus based models, Haiku generation in particular has been a target for vector space model approaches to computational poetry. Gaiku (Netzer et al., 2009), for instance, uses a combination of human generated word association norms and sequences of syntax derived from a statistical analysis of a corpus of existing haiku to generate new haiku which are designed to be as meaningful, grammatical, and poetic as possible. The First Sally system for Haiku generation (Droog-Hayes and Wiggins, 2015) uses a distributional semantic model, based on an analysis of word co-occurrences in a large scale textual corpus, to generate sets of conceptually related words, and in this regard is closely related to the semantic element of the new system described in Section 3.1.

Of particular interest to the study presented here is the system for poetry generation based on the FACE model for assessing computational creativity (Colton et al., 2012). This model focuses on the evaluation of creativity associated not just with assessment of the artefact generated by the system, but also with observation of the process which the system undertakes to produce its output. With regard to poetry in particular, the model architects are concerned with the critical conveyance of "communicative purpose" (p. 96) which is essential to the understanding of linguistic expression: as consumers of poetry, we rely on the belief that something more than just a random or cleverly constrained but decontextualised process lies at the other end of the poem itself. In short, we count on meaning being anchored in intent.

In the case of the poetic implementation of the FACE model, this has meant that poems are coupled with expository statements regarding data analysis that has served as a situation specific motivation for the generation of each poem. The system itself operates by way of template completion, inserting into prefigured lines of verse similes mined from the web using a pattern fitting heuristic to determine viable word combinations. In order to convey a sense of intent to its output, the system weights the phrases it extracts from the web based on a sentiment analysis, seeking to choose similes which correspond in sentiment with a similarly analysed selection of text from a current newspaper. The idea here is that, by rooting the poem in the mood of a currently or recently unfolding event, the system's output becomes tied to something happening in the world, and the reader becomes more committed to the idea that the computer is an agent creating an artefact in reaction to a situation. In particular, the system frames its explanation as a first-person exposition involving an analysis of the mood of the news on a given day, with a degree of justification for this analysis: the system presents itself as a willful actor knowingly engaged in a creative, interpretive process.

Our hypothesis is that the system based on the FACE model, when it comes to the evaluation of computer generated poetry, has got it at least half right, in that the perception of a creative procedure underlying the computational generation of poetry is a crucial factor in the creative quality of the poetic artefact. And one way to convey a creative procedure is to couch the operation of the computer in a narrative of the machine having a self-reflective sense of goal-directedness, a kind of transparent fiction of agency exploiting the human tendency to read intentions and beliefs into all sorts of situations in the world where we know there actually are none (Carruthers, 2011). We believe, though, that readers of poetry are at this stage in the history of technology and art prepared to engage with computer produced verse in a more frank way, acknowledging the statistical character of the underlying operation without losing regard for the inherent degree of creativity, and in fact possibly taking the output more seriously when the generative procedure is presented in a straightforward, objective manner.

3   Autonomous and Contextual Poetry

In order to evaluate human assessment of both creative process and output, we have designed a relatively straightforward system for generating short, loosely constrained poems. This system has been designed with three critical principles in mind:

- The system uses a machine learning technique for the unsupervised generation of semantic relationships.

- The semantic relationships which serve as one of the constraints on the systems output are context sensitive, and in this way can be associated with *ad hoc* input allowing the poems to be *about* something topical.

- The system uses a statistical technique to constrain the phonology of the poem, and so is designed to produce text that sounds poetic.

Over the course of this section, we'll lay out a series of models which are algoritmically concatenated into a system which seeks to fulfill these requirement.

3.1   A Semantic Model

At its root this system is based on a statistical model of word meaning constructed within the distributional semantic paradigm, construing words as vectors within a space of dimensions representing co-occurrences with other words over the course of a large-scale textual corpus (Turney and Patel, 2010; Clark, 2015). The key feature of this particular model is its context sensitivity: it dynamically generates new semantic spaces based on an analysis of the conceptual relationships between a set of input terms (McGregor et al., 2015; Agres et al., 2015).

The objective of this component of the poetry generating system is to generate spaces in which the conceptual relationships between words

The motivation for using this particular model is twofold. For one thing, the model derives its features from an unsupervised traversal of a corpus, so the semantic relationships which it captures are discovered without the human dictated assignment of symbol manipulating rules. This property ostensibly gives the poetry generating system at least a semblance of agency. And, on the other hand, the dynamic, contextual component of the model enables it to engage with *ad hoc* input, allowing the model to generate output topically related to other textual artefacts. This means there is some hope of conveying a sense of intentionality or aboutness to an observer of the system's process.

This semantic model is based on a very high-dimensional (approximately 7.5 million), very sparse space of word-vectors generated from a traversal of the English language component of Wikipedia. The dimensions of this space correspond to terms that co-occur in sentences with words from the model's 200,000 word vocabulary. The value for each dimension is based on a pointwise mutual information metric derived as follows, where $n_{w,c}$ corresponds to the frequency with which vocabulary word w co-occurs with context word c, W is the overall count of vocabulary word tokens, n_w and n_c are the respective independent frequencies of w and c, and a is a smoothing constant:

$$M_{w,c} = \log_2 \left(\frac{n_{w,c} \times W}{n_w \times (n_c + a)} + 1 \right) \quad (1)$$

The sparse space generated through this process can be reduced to a context dependent, conceptually oriented subspace through an analsyis of a set of input terms. So, for instance, in a 200 dimensional subspace based on co-occurrence dimensions salient to the words `cat`, `dog`, and `goldfish`, `cat` is closest to the words like `rabbit`, `hamster`, and `pet`. If, on the other hand, we build a subspace based on the input words `cat`, `lion`, and `tiger`, `cat` becomes proximate to words like `leopard`, `hyena`, and `wild`. Technical details for generating subspaces are laid out in detail in (McGregor et al., 2015).

3.2 A Phonological Model

This process of building a space of potential sub-spaces is coupled with a phonological model which similarly uses an information theoretic metric to try to capture the way in which word-sounds are expected to co-occur in poetry. This model is also constructed from a statistical model of a corpus, in this instance a corpus containing about 1500 English language sonnets.[1] These sonnets are rendered into a format containing both phonemic and syllabic information, based on a syllabified version of the CMU Arpabet (Bartlett et al., 2009). Frequencies of phonemic co-occurrence $C_i(p_a, p_b)$ are then tabulated, where the count C is the total number of times phoneme p_b occurs i syllables in front of phoneme p_b in a line of a poem. Once all frequencies for all lines in all poems in the corpus are compiled, these statistics are converted into mutual information measures, formulated here with $C_i(T)$ representing the total number of phonemes occurring i syllables apart and $C_i(p_a)$ and $C_{-i}(p_b)$ standing for the independent frequencies at which phonemes p_a and p_b occur i or $-i$ syllables away respectively from any other syllable:

$$P_i(p_a, p_b) = \log_2 \left(\frac{C_i(p_a, p_b) C_i(T)}{C_i(p_a) C_{-i}(p_b)} + 1 \right) \quad (2)$$

From this matrix of phoneme-distance relationships, a score can be generated for the phonological strength of any two given candidate syllables s_1 and s_2 potentially occurring in a line of poetry generated by the system, where l_1 and l_2 are the respective lengths of s_1 and s_2, and p_1 and p_2 are corresponding constituent phonemes:

$$S_i(s_1, s_2) = \frac{1}{l_1 l_2} \times \sum_{p_1=1}^{l_1} \sum_{p_2=1}^{l_2} P_i(p_1, p_2) \quad (3)$$

This phonological model is incorporated into our poetry generating system in order to impose a sense of prosody on the output. As with the semantic model, there are no phonetic or metric constraints hand-coded by human designers, and so we can claim that, to the degree that prosodic features do emerge in the system's output, these elements are discovered by the system itself as statistical properties inherent to the underlying corpus of sonnets.

3.3 A Syntactic Model

The third constraint placed on our poetry generating system consists of an n-gram model for stringing together parts of speech in ostensibly syntactic ways. Statistics are once again harvested from the corpus of about 1,500 English language sonnets, in this case with each word tagged with a part of speech label using the Python Natural Language Toolkit word tokeniser.[2] Once these tagged renditions of the corpus are generated, a probabilistic model for predicting the syntactic continuation of a string of parts of speech is built, describe here with $n_{t,q}$ representing the frequency with which part of speech t follows the sequence of parts of speech q in a line of poetry, and n_q signifying the total number of times the sequence q is observed in any line:

$$G(t|q) = \frac{n_{t,q}}{n_q} \quad (4)$$

If, in the course of generating a line verse, the system generates a sequence q that has no observed extension, is will remove the first element in q to produce sequence q' and will then generate element t with probability $G(t|q')$. The purpose of this operation is to impose an arguably superficial element of grammaticality on the system's output. Anecdotally, but also significantly, professional poets who have interacted with the system have actually suggested that this component of the process over-constrains the output to the detriment of the interesting conceptual and phonological relationships generated by the other models.[3] Nonetheless, for the purpose of the comparative study presented here, this component of the system is maintained. Also of note is that this syntactic model is the only component of the system that simulates a non-deterministic process.

3.4 Sentiment Analysis

The final aspect of the poetry generating system is a model for analysing the sentiment of a document

---

[1] www.sonnets.org.

[2] www.nltk.org/_modules/nltk/tokenize.html

[3] In the course of the Globe Road Poetry Festival at Queen Mary in November 2015 and the Portrait of the Machine as a Young Artist event at the British Library in February 2016.

within a corpus. In the case of the poems used for the study here, the corpus in question is the Penn Treebank Switchboard corpus, consisting of 1,126 transcribed telephone conversations.[4] A straightforward term frequency-inverse document frequency technique is employed in order to create a topic model for each conversation within the corpus (Salton and McGill, 1983). Specifically, for a given document (conversation) d, the words representing the salient topics of the conversation are ranked according to this equation, where w is a word that occurs within the document, w_d is the number of times w appears in d, and w_c is the number of times w occurs in the entire corpus of conversations:

$$T(d, w) = \frac{w_d}{w_c} \tag{5}$$

For each conversation in the corpus, the top four topical terms based on the above equation are selected, and the sentiment of these terms is rated along a negative-positive spectrum. The rating for a given word is derived from the SentiWordNet database of word sentiment scores, which assigns negative and positive ratings to senses of a large number of words.[5] In order to rank the sentiment of each conversation, each word is assigned the mean score of its various sentences, and then the average scores of the four most salient terms is taken to give each conversation an overall ranking.

The purpose of analysing the sentiment of a transcribed conversation is to give the poetry generating system a topic as a topical handle, allowing the poem to be about something specific and intersubjective. The idea, following on from (Colton et al., 2012), is that a poem that is endowed with intentionality is more likely to be deemed as creative by an observer.

3.5   Assembling a Poem

Finally, the various modular components described above are linked together to algorithmically generate poems for subsequent analysis by human readers according to the following procedure:

1. The 17 most negative and 16 most positive conversations, ranked as described in Section 3.4, are selected as topics for poems.

2. The four topics of each conversation are fed into the semantic model describe in Section 3.1. A subspace of conceptually related words is generated, with the salient region of this space considered that which is closest to the mean of the topical input terms. The words in this subspace are tagged with their most likely part of speech.

3. A syntactic string is probabilistically generated based on Equation 4, and a line of poetry of no more than 11 syllables is correspondingly composed.

4. At each step in the generative process, the word that is closest to the salient region of the space described in Step 2, aside from the input terms themselves, that matches the next part of speech prescribed by Step 3 is choosen as a continuation of the line being composed. A base poem of four lines is generated.

5. Each word in each line is given a score of phonological appropriateness based on the average score of each of its syllables compared with all other syllables in the line, including the other syllables in the word itself. This phonological score is then multiplied by $1 - (z \times sent(w))$, where $sent(w)$ is the sentimental rating of word w according to the SentiWordNet database, while the value of z is -1 if the overall sentiment of the input terms is negative and +1 if the prevalent sentiment is positive.

6. The least appropriate word in the poem is removed and replaced with the most appropriate word, selected from a vocabulary defined in terms of the 1,000 most conceptually salient words as established in the subspace derived in Step 2. Steps 5 and 6 are repeated until the poem converges to a maximally scored state.

The final product of this process is intended to be a poem which is conceptually relevant to the conversation serving as the basis for the input terms while exhibiting poetic phonology, sentiment appropriate to the input topic, and a modicum of grammaticality.

---

[4] www.cis.upenn.edu/~treebank/
[5] http://sentiwordnet.isti.cnr.it/

4 Evaluation of Process and Product

Based on the generative process described throughout Section 3, 33 poems have been randomly generated, each associated with a conversation summarised by the four words derived through the technique described in Section 3.4. We have subsequently generated three different versions of these poems, one prefaced with a brief objective description of the generative process, one prefaced with a brief subjective description framing the system as a self-aware agent, and one with no preface at all. An example of the objective preface is as follows:

This poem is based on a sentimental and conceptual analysis of a conversation containing words like 'sickening', 'shitty', 'novice', and 'hack'. The sentimental component of the analysis determined the conversation was negative. The poem emerged as a pathway in a space of word points derived from this statistical analysis, with an additional criterion for selecting poetic sounding combinations of words.

And the subjective description of the same poem reads as follows:

I listened to a conversation containing words like 'sickening', 'shitty', 'novice', and 'hack'. I considered this to be a negative conversation. I decided to write a poem about this conversation, and have tried to capture some of the negative sentiment while also focusing on how the poem sounds.

Finally, the poem that accompanies these descriptions reads like this:

and wondered but talked me shifty Sinatra
like hang says in current or that four man
because this full gets really there makes both
another golden way though your man

We constructed a survey consisting of a total of 99 poems: each of the 33 poems our system generated, with each of the three versions of the explanatory preface (or lack thereof). Each survey participant was first presented with a introduction page laying out the survey, informing them that they would be reading a poem generated by a computer and then asked to evaluate the poem. On the next page, the

	creativity	meaningful	quality
obj	3.14 (*1.88*)	1.67 (*0.78*)	2.05 (*1.05*)
subj	2.93 (*1.63*)	2.00 (*1.32*)	2.07 (*0.96*)
none	2.93 (*1.60*)	1.54 (*0.63*)	2.14 (*1.33*)

Table 1: Mean scores along a seven-point scale (with standard deviations in parentheses) for human subject evaluations of creativity, meaningfulness, and quality of computer generated poems prefaced with an objective description of the generative process, a subjective description, or no description at all.

poem itself was presented, preceded by either one of the two types of procedural descriptions illustrated above or by no description at all. On the same page, subjects were asked to evaluate the poem they had just read based on three different criteria: *creativity*, *meaningfulness*, and *quality*, in each case giving the poem a rating along a seven point scale ranging from "low" to "high". Finally the subjects were presented with a third page where they were asked to provide optional information about their age and their self-assessed proficiency or knowledge in the English language, poetry, and computer science, again in each case rating themselves along a seven-point scale, in these instances ranging from "novice" to "expert".

We received responses from 79 participants, with each participant evaluating a unique preface-poem combination. Reported ages ranged from 20 to 72, with a mean of 40. The mean value for proficiency in English was 6.26, with standard deviation of 0.92; for knowledge of poetry, the mean was 4.12 with stdv of 1.46; for knowledge of computer science, the mean was 4.66, with stdv of 1.96. The mean responses, along with standard deviations, are presented in Table 4.

The overall picture these results paint is that, in the case of the type of poetry being generated by our system, the mode of presentation has a marginal effect on the evaluation of content. The higher value of creativity typically accorded to poems presented with an objective description correlates with our hypothesis that readers would react favourably to this transparent presentation of process, by the difference between this value and the mean creativity assigned to poems subjectively framed is not statistically significant: a two-tailed Student's t-test on the results gives a p-value of 0.68 and a t-value of

0.42. The relatively similar mean scores, combined with high degrees of standard deviation, indicate that these results, at least in terms of a comparison between the data for each type of presentation, aren't distinguishable from what we would expect if subjects randomly assigned values to poems.

Also of not is the relatively high scores given to the subjectively presented poems in terms of the meaningfulness of the poems. Statistical significance is slightly higher here, with a p-value of 0.31 and a t-value of 1.02, but still hardly noteworthy. The one thing that does perhaps bear further consideration here is the way that subjects seem relatively comfortable ascribing creativity to poems presented as products of statistical processes versus the meaningfulness attributed to poems framed as subjective experiences of information in and about the world. Perhaps the appropriate interpretation here is that readers appreciate the insight into the productive mechanism afforded by the objective presentation, and associate this with creativity, whereas meaningfulness is more closely connected to the impression of agency and individuation conveyed by the subjective presentation.

Finally, it is also worth mentioning that the poems presented with no procedural description at all do just about as well as the lesser of the two explained poems in terms of creativity and meaningfulness, and actually do slightly better than the other two types in terms of quality. Quality is arguably a somewhat vague category, and was intended to cover a range of properties such as poeticness and composition. On the whole, though, the story here seems to be that, at least in terms of this type of poetry, with the relatively cursory kind of procedural description we were able to offer in the course of a survey that was, by design, quite brief, the way that the poems are presented doesn't make a big difference in terms of how humans rate this type of output.

5 Conclusion

Further to the brief analysis offered above, another point of interest with this study relates to the relatively high degree of standard deviation evident across all the results. The story here would seem to be that there is a wide range of opinion on how exactly computer generated poetry should be evaluated

in the first place. Anecdotally, responses in most categories for most types of presentation ranged from one to seven, despite all of the 33 poems being of a generally similar quality. There seems to be a lack of consensus regarding how to consider computers as poets.

This analysis aligns with the feedback received in the course of the the events involving engagement between human poets and computational systems for poetry generation mentioned in Section 3.3. Specifically, a self-selecting group of technologically receptive poets found much value in engaging with the system described here, which they saw as a mechanism for discovering interesting, novel, and potentially productive conceptual concordances within a corpus which were obscure to a human reader but nonetheless poetically valuable. This approach to poetry as an artefact of a dynamic engagement between poets, readers, corpora, society, and the environment is conducive to the type of poetry generated by our system—but this particular aesthetic stance is hardly universal in the world of poetry readers.

Compared to the output of the Full FACE system, the output of our system is, more or less objectively, more garbled and less structured. On the other hand, the FACE system resorts to heuristic simile mining and template filling, where our system maintains a somewhat higher degree of autonomy in its analysis of a corpus and dynamic projection of conceptually loaded semantic subspaces. Whether readers provided with more comprehensive descriptions of the differences between these approaches would consider one system more creative than the other remains to be seen, and is beside the point of the study presented here, which has been a first attempt at assessing whether or not the way that the creative process involved in the computational production of poetry is framed has a significant impact on evaluation of output.

Returning to our earlier discussion of creativity as a phenomenon dynamically distributed across a society and an environment, we ultimately expect evaluations of creativity to take into account various factors integrating the overall situation of an artefact. So, for instance, in the case of poetry, we would predict that the relationship between a poem, its mode of production, and the milieu in which the poem is produced should all contribute to the assessment of the inherent creativity, quality, and meaningfulness of both the poem itself and the poetic act. Similar insight seems to have motivated the implementation of the FACE model that has been discussed here, which seeks to act as an agent of both generation and interpretation. While the study described in this paper has focused on the effect of procedural description on poetic evaluation, we might conjecture that the dynamically context-sensitive model that provides the conceptual component of our system is the right kind of computational process to offer a compelling platform for environmental situatedness.

The criteria for evaluating creativity discussed here, construed in terms of three values and presented to study participants without any further explanation, admittedly offer a relatively blunt approach to judging the merit of computational output, let alone to assessing the more general creative process and the relationship between this process and its situation in the world. In the future, in addition to improvements to the system itself, further advances to this work would involve the construction of an evaluative mechanism which incorporates a more complete description of the system's operation and environmental situation, as well as a more nuanced range of questions to enrich the evaluative process. For now, the outcome seems to be that there is still too varied an attitude towards what it means for a computer to claim creative autonomy for there to be a meaningful consensus on the merit of poetic output based on a relatively straightforward encounter with a poetry generating computer.

Acknowledgments

This research has been supported by EPSRC grant EP/L50483X/1. The project ConCreTe acknowledges the financial support of the Future and Emerging Technologies (FET) programme within the Seventh Framework Programme for Research of the European Commission, under FET grant number 611733.

References

Kat Agres, Stephen McGregor, Matthew Purver, and Geraint Wiggins. 2015. Conceptualising creativity: From distributional semantics to conceptual spaces. In *Proceedings of the 6th International Conference on Computational Creativity*, Park City, UT.

Lawrence W. Barsalou. 2008. Grounded cognition. *Annual Review of Psychology*, 59:617–645.

Susan Bartlett, Grzegorz Kondrak, and Colin Cherry. 2009. On the syllabification of phonemes. *Proceedings of Human Language Technologies: The Annual Conference of the North American Chapter of the Association for Computational Linguistics*, pages 308–316.

Margaret A. Boden. 1990. *The Creative Mind: Myths and Mechanisms*. Weidenfeld and Nicolson, London.

Peter Carruthers. 2011. *The Opacity of Mind: An Integrative Theory of Self-Knowledge*. Oxford University Press.

Stephen Clark. 2015. Vector space models of lexical meaning. In Shalom Lappin and Chris Fox, editors, *The Handbook of Contemporary Semantic Theory*. Wiley-Blackwell.

Simon Colton and Geraint Wiggins. 2012. Computational creativity: The final frontier? In *Proceedings of the 21st European Conference on Artificial Intelligence*.

Simon Colton, Jacob Goodwin, and Tony Veale. 2012. Full-FACE poetry generation. *Proceedings of the Third International Conference on Computational Creativity*, pages 95–102.

Max Droog-Hayes and Geraint A. Wiggins. 2015. Improved meaning in poetry using statistical methods. In *Proceedings of the Sixth International Conference on Computational Creativity*.

Pablo Gervás. 2000. Wasp: Evaluation of different strategies for the automatic generation of spanish verse. In *Proceedings of the AISB-00 Symposium on Creative & Cultural Aspects of AI*, pages 93–100.

Anna Jordanous. 2015. Four pppperspectives on computational creativity. In *Proceedings of AISB 2015s Second International Symposium on Computational Creativity*.

Stephen McGregor, Kat Agres, Matthew Purver, and Geraint Wiggins. 2015. From distributional semantics to conceptual spaces: A novel computational method for concept creation. *Journal of Artificial General Intelligence*.

Yael Netzer, David Gabay, Yoav Goldberg, and Michael Elhadad. 2009. Gaiku : Generating haiku with word associations norms. In *Proceedings of the NAACL HLT Workshop on Computational Approaches to Linguistic Creativity*, pages 32–39.

Hugo Gonçalo Oliveira. 2012. PoeTryMe: A versatile platform for poetry generation. In *Proceedings of the ECAI 2012 Workshop on Computational Creativity, Concept Invention, and General Intelligence*.

Graeme Ritchie. 2012. A closer look at creativity as search. In *Proceedings of the 2012 International Conference on Computational Creativity*.

Gerard Salton and Michael J. McGill. 1983. *Introduction to Modern Information Retrieval*. McGraw-Hill Book Company, New York, NY.

Kenny Smith, Henry Brighton, and Simon Kirby. 2003. Complex systems in language evolution: The cultural emergence of compositional structure. *Advances in Complex Systems*, 06(04):537–558.

Jukka Toivanen, Hannu Toivonen, Alessandro Valitutti, and Oskar Gross. 2012. Corpus-based generation of content and form in poetry. In *Proceedings of the Third International Conference on Computational Creativity*, pages 175–179.

Peter D. Turney and Patrick Patel. 2010. From frequency to meaning: Vector space models of semantics. *Journal of Artificial Intelligence Research*, 37:141–188.

Combinatorics vs Grammar:
archeology of computational poetry in *Tape Mark I*

Alessandro Mazzei[+] and **Andrea Valle**[*]
[+]Dipartimento di Informatica [*]Dipartimento di Studi Umanistici
CIRMA: Centro Interdipartimentale di Ricerca Sulla Multimedialità e l'Audiovisivo
Università degli Studi di Torino
`[alessandro.mazzei|andrea.valle]@unito.it`

Abstract

The paper presents a reconstruction of the automatic poetry generation system realized in Italy in 1961 by Nanni Balestrini to compose the poem *Tape Mark I*. The major goal of the paper is to provide a critical comparison between the high-level approach that seems to be suggested by the poet, and the low-level combinatorial algorithm that was actually implemented. This comparison allows to assess the relevance of how the available technology constrained and shaped the work of the poet, to reveal some of his aesthetic assumptions, and to discuss some aspects of the relation between human and the machine in the creative process.

1 Introduction

Systems for automatic poetry generation (APG) introduce specific features when compared to systems for natural language generation (NLG). While most of data-to-text NLG systems usually follow a pipeline architecture (Reiter, 2007), a number of different architectures and techniques have been applied in APG (Gervás, Pablo, 2015). A crucial difference between APG and NLG is the nature of the input, that unavoidably involves its evaluation. The evaluation of a NLG system can be based on a reference corpus, on human evaluation or on the execution of a given task. However, all these evaluation strategies rely on the reception/comprehension of the message, that is, on the meaning units contained in the input. In contrast, in the case of APG, a clear notion of input content is not clearly available, and the evaluation of the output is an opaque task,

as it depends on aesthetic (or more largely, cultural), widely variable assumptions. In this sense, APG are similar to other context-evaluated linguistic phenomena such as metaphors. An example of quantitative evaluation of APG based on human judgments is reported in (Toivanen et al., 2012).

By following the classification proposed in (Gervas, 2016), there are two main categories of APG systems: the first category is composed by systems that reuse fragments of text from other poetic texts; the second category is composed by systems that generate a stream of text by using some procedures that exploit word-to-word relations. APG systems from both these categories may use different kinds of linguistic information since fragments fusion, as well as word-to-word relations, can be based on lexical, morpho-syntactical, semantic, rhetorical or metrical theories. Indeed, fragments fusion can be modeled as a string-based fusion in relation to some combinatorial procedure or, in alternative, as a more complex grammar-based fusion, in this case accounting for more sophisticated linguistic theories. Only the detailed analysis of a certain specific APG system, rooted on a reproducible implementation, i.e. algorithms and data structures, can help us to understand the real linguistic creative nature of the poetic generation process involved. Another important component in the analysis of the creative aspects of an APG concerns the non-algorithmic contribution that the poet-programmer may introduce in the final version of the poetic artwork. Indeed, often the poet-programmer, especially in the earlier years of APG, modifies the output provided by the APG system in order to solve some linguistic issues of

Proceedings of the INLG 2016 Workshop on Computational Creativity and Natural Language Generation, pages 61–70,
Edinburgh, September 2016. ©2016 Association for Computational Linguistics

the system, or in order to select one among various possible outputs (Funkhouser and Baldwin, 2007).

The aim of this paper is to perform an experiment in *archeology of multimedia* (Lombardo et al., 2006): we first analyze, and then reproduce, the poem *Tape Mark I* by strictly following the actually implemented algorithm (Balestrini, 1962). *Tape Mark I* was a pioneering example of APG dating from 1961, implemented in the assembler of an IBM 7070, one of the first commercial fully transistorized computer. By reproducing the original algorithm we have been able to understand: (1) the details of the creative process related to the combinatorial fusion of textual fragments; (2) the real contribution given by the human poet to the final version of the artwork.

The rest of the paper is organized as follows: Section 2 historically introduces *Tape Mark I*; Section 3 and Section 4 report the computational descriptions of the artwork from, respectively, a high- and low-level perspective; Section 5 describes a simulation experiment regarding the poem; Section 6 critically considers the relation between the author and the algorithm; Section 7 adds some critical conclusions on the evaluation of the system.

2 Balestrini and computer-generated poetry

Funkhauser has reconstructed a chronology of the first attempts in computer-generated poetry (Funkhouser and Baldwin, 2007):

1959: Theo Lutz (a student of the theorist of Information aesthetics Max Bense) implements the first programs for computing poems, *Stochastische Texte* (a text generator);

1960: the French *Oulipo* group is founded (including the notorious writers Queneau and Perec, but also mathematicians, that were mostly concerned with combinatorial approaches from an anti-lyrical perspective);

1960: Brion Gysin composes his permutation poem *I am that I am*, programmed by Ian Somerville;

1961: Nanni Balestrini produces *Tape Mark I* on an IBM 7070;

1961: Rul Gunzenhäuser composes *Weinachtgedicht* (automatic poems).

Thus, *Tape Mark I* is one of the first examples of the use of a computer to generate poetry (Balestrini,

1962; Balestrini, 1968). In 1961 Balestrini (born 1935), while still a young poet, was already a fundamental figure in the Italian avantgarde movement. His poems were included in the crucial anthology *I novissimi* [the newest] (Giuliani, 1961) and he later became a member of the experimental collective *Gruppo '63* (Alicicco et al., 2010). In his long and still continuing career, he has also been the recipient of a prize at Venice Biennale for his visual work, still related to the manipulation of language. Since its inception, Balestrini's work provided a specific version of the main aesthetic assumption theorized by *novissimi* –language as a material reality on which the poet operates– through the extensive manipulation of textual fragments by other authors, retrieved from disparate sources, e.g. novels, essays, poetry, newspapers, popular magazines. This kind of technique, that can be associated to the cutup processes by W. Burroughs and to other collage-based avantgarde approaches (Renello, 2010), was at the basis of *Tape Mark I*, and was to be developed further by the author, leading him to write an entirely computer-generated novel, *Tristano* (1966, (Balestrini, 2016)). The relevance of the poem was immediately recognized internationally as *Tape Mark I* was featured in the first exhibition dedicated (1968) to electronic and computer art, *Cybernetic Serendipity* (Reichardt, 1968; MacGregor, 2002; Boden, 2015).

3 *Tape Mark I*: high-level model

Tape Mark I was included and extensively documented in the *Almanacco Bompiani 1962*, a yearly publication by Bompiani publisher since 1925, that in that year issued a special volume dedicated to the "application of computers to moral sciences and literature" (Morando, 1962). The contribution by Balestrini featured the poem, a description of the generative procedure, information on the implementation and the relative outputs.

Tape Mark I starts from three fragments ("groups") extracted from the following texts (here we report the Italian titles of the first two):

1. *Diario di Hiroshima* by Michihito Hachiya
2. *Il mistero dell'ascensore* by Paul Goldwin
3. *Tao te King, XVI*, by Lao Tse

Figure 1 shows the three groups. Each line is an "element" subdivided into "metrical units" (/) and provided with one "head code" (*codice di testa*) and one "tail code" (*codice di coda*), respectively on the right and left side. Numbers are not to be read as fractions, rather they represent couples of input and output codes. The *Almanacco* provides a set of four

Testo

Codice di testa		Codice di coda
I (da *Diario di Hiroshima* di Michihito Hachiya)		
1/4	l'accecante / globo / di fuoco	2/3
1/2	si espande / rapidamente	3/4
2/3	trenta volte / piú luminoso / del sole	2/4
3/4	quando raggiunge / la stratosfera	1/2
1/3	la sommità / della nuvola	2/3
2/4	assume / la ben nota forma / di fungo	3/4
II (da *Il mistero dell'ascensore* di Paul Goldwin)		
1/4	la testa / premuta / sulla spalla	2/4
1/4	i capelli / tra le labbra	2/4
2/3	giacquero / immobili / senza parlare	2/3
3/4	finché non mosse / le dita / lentamente	1/3
3/4	cercando / di afferrare	1/2
III (da *Tao te King*, XVI, di Laotse)		
1/2	mentre la moltitudine / delle cose / accade	1/2
2/3	io contemplo / il loro ritorno	3/4
1/2	malgrado / che le cose / fioriscano	2/3
2/3	esse tornano / tutte / alla loro radice	1/4

Figure 1: Source text organization in groups.

"instructions" that allow to generate *Tape Mark I* (and, in the poet's ideas, possibly other poems) from the groups (Balestrini, 1968):

I. Make combinations of ten elements out of the given fifteen, without permutations or repetitions.

II. Construct chains of elements taking into account the head-codes and tail-codes

III. Avoid juxtaposing elements drawn from the same extract (i.e. group).

IV. Subdivide the chains of ten elements into six lines of four metrical units each.

The algorithm reported the instructions in natural language without any specifications about the data structures. Step I introduces a constraint that is totally opaque at this point (we will discuss it later). Step II indicates how to sequence the elements. As an example, an element ending with a tail code $= 1/2$ can be concatenated only with elements having 1 or 2 as head code. Step III specifies a constraint on sequencing, as only elements coming from different groups may be concatenated. Step IV is a grouping operation on the resulting sequence. Here "metrical units" come into play, as the final chain is subdivided into verses made up of 4 metrical units (again, the number 10 is mysterious, more on this later). The final poem has to be a sort of sestina (Brancaleoni, 2007), as it is made up of six stanzas of six lines. In order to study the system as pro-

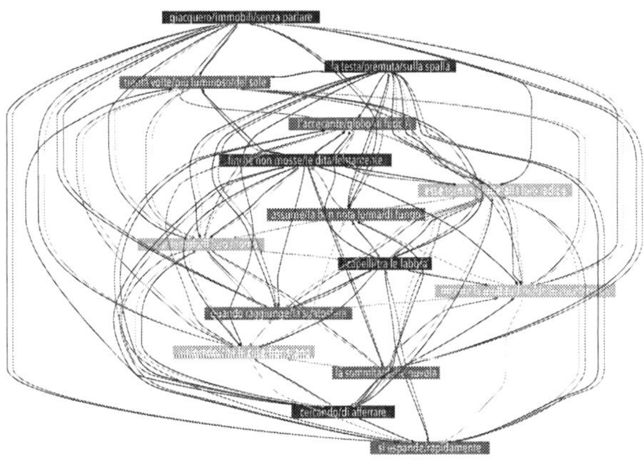

Figure 2: *Tape Mark I* graph.

posed by the "instructions", we first implemented a program based on a graph model, as instructions define each element as having two predecessor and two successors in the set of the 15 elements.

Figure 2 shows a plotting by the Graphviz package of the graph that results from the data structure of predecessors/successors. Vertices represent elements, their color indicate the group they belong to, edges link to successors, their color being related to the predecessor. The graph is a direct, cyclic graph, and while not totally connected, it still does not reveal a specific topology (e.g. it is not a power law

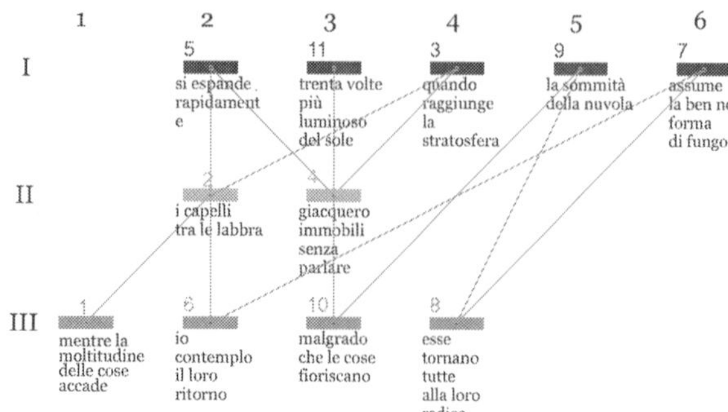

Figure 3: *Tape Mark I* as a path on a graph.

graph, where some vertices are densely connected). Such a topology seems to suggest a sort of uniform distribution of the elements, that more or less share the same rank. The graph represents all the virtual sequencing possibilities of the system as it takes into account also the Step II constraint on adjacent elements from different groups. An automatic visualization (using the Python-based Nodebox package) of a possible poem as a path on the graph is shown in Figure 3, where the vertical axis represents groups (the group is an attribute of vertices), the horizontal one represents elements, and each vertex is labeled on top with the sequence index (starting from 1 in group III, element 3).

Such a modelization by means of a graph defines a possible syntax, and explicitly aims at introducing a generative perspective, where each path on the graph is a possible poem. Being the graph cyclic, theoretically a path can be infinite, and the same vertices may be traversed more times. Here Step I comes into play, as it states (but this can be assessed only taking into account the implementation, as we will see) that no repetitions are possible. So Figure 3 shows a path with no repetitions, as vertices –once traversed– are no more available. This constraint results in various valid paths for a maximum of 15 vertices, the shortest valid paths having length $= 8$. Indeed, the graph model reported in Figure 2 can be thought as a grammar, as it falls in the set of the regular grammars in the Chomsky hierarchy, i.e. the simplest form of generative grammar, which is equivalent, in the recognition process, to a finite state automaton (Hopcroft et al., 2006). Such a simple grammar modelization poses an interesting question: was Balestrini in need of a computer?

By drawing a graph on a paper sheet, the handmade generation of sequences is not a big deal. The key point is that Balestrini is not thinking in terms of a grammar-based model[1]. So, even if Balestrini's algorithm as provided by the "instructions" can be easily modeled as a generative procedure, it was not thought in these terms. Rather than in a generative, syntactic fashion, Balestrini was thinking in a combinatorial one. The graph model indicates that the maximum length of a sequence is 15. But the final poem is much longer (six stanzas of six verses). This can be understood only by inspecting the low level algorithm, that explains instruction I.

4   *Tape Mark I*: low-level model

Apart from the "instructions" section, the description of *Tape Mark I* reported in the *Almanacco Bompiani* (Morando, 1962) contains a section called *Elaborazione del Calcolatore* [computer processing]. It shows a complex flowchart (see Figure 4) that was probably completely opaque to the readers and intended only to document the "esoteric" low-level machine level, while the plain language "instructions" were its "exoteric", high-level side. Nevertheless, the flowchart allowed us for a more precise reconstruction of the original system[2].

The original program for *Tape Mark I* was written in the IBM 7070 assembler called AUTOCODER (IBM, 1961). From the description and by inspecting the flowchart of the low-level algorithm, we can reconstruct the memory organization adopted by the programmer (the engineer Alberto Nobis). The memory was organized in four tables, called Table-A, Table-B, Table-C and, not mentioned in the text, Table-(d) (see Figure 5). Table-A contains the original text fragments, i.e. each cell contains an element $(1 \rightarrow 15)$. A notable consequence is that each cell has a variable length. Table-B contains pointers, i.e. each cell contains two pointers to the beginning and to the end positions in Table-A (in Table-B, Bn and En respectively indicating BEGIN and END), of a specific element. Table-C contains four

---

[1]It might be noted that Chomsky's *Syntactic structures* was published only four years before (1957). Nevertheless, Balestrini (Morando, 1962) explicitly mentions grammars as a future reference for his work.

[2]Other information on the technical aspects, probably from an interview to Nobis, are reported by (Comai, 1985).

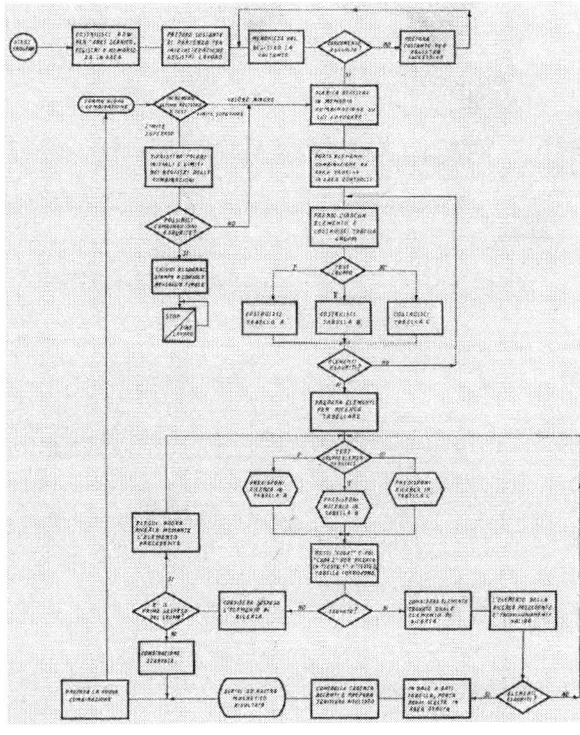

Figure 4: Flowchart by A. Nobis showing the memory procedures for table filling and result testing in the AUTOCODER implementation.

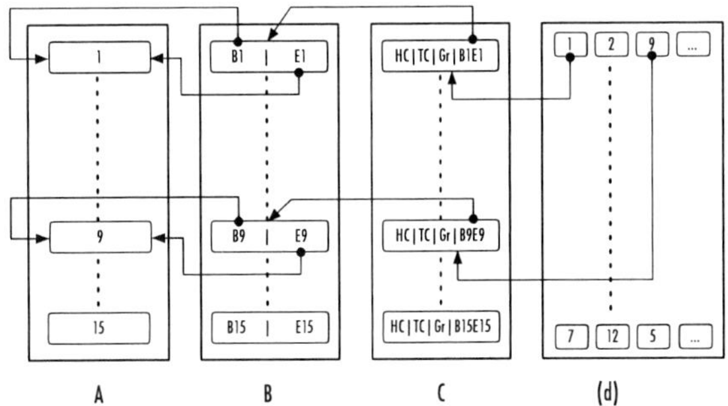

Figure 5: Memory organization of *Tape Mark I* implemented algorithm.

Here the number 10 comes into play, the one that was mysteriously mentioned by Balestrini in the "instructions". It is not clear why Balestrini introduces this constraint, and both aesthetic (high-level) and technical (low-level, due to pressing memory constraints on the IBM 7070) explanations are possible. This means that the whole process at each run takes into account (and generates) a 10−element sequence. This memory organization probably also explains why elements are always provided with two head and two tail codes. The latter feature may be seen as a feedback constraint from low- to high-level (i.e. the "instructions"). To have a variable number of head and tail codes would have meant to define a further pointer table to take into account their variable length.

5 The simulation experiment

The flowchart in Figure 6 is the conceptual schema of *Tape Mark I* and formalizes the steps performed both by the human ("author") and by the machine. In step I ("Generation"), the algorithm starts from

distinct data: (i) the head code of a specific element (HC); (ii) the tail code of the element (TC); (iii) the group to which the fragment belongs to (Gr); (iv) the position in Table-B of the pointer (BnEn). Finally, Table-(d) contains the combination of the positions of the Table-C, which correspond to the combination that has been initially extracted from a permutation of 10 over 15 elements. That is, Table-(d) contains a serie of indexes $[1, \ldots 15]$ that represents the elements to be permuted at the initialization phase of each cycle.

By this organization of the memory we understand that the low-level algorithm essentially works on pointers, i.e. the permutation of the fragments essentially consists of a permutation of memory positions of Table-C, and each possible combination extracted from this permutation is essentially a sequence of 10 positions (pointers) of the Table-C.

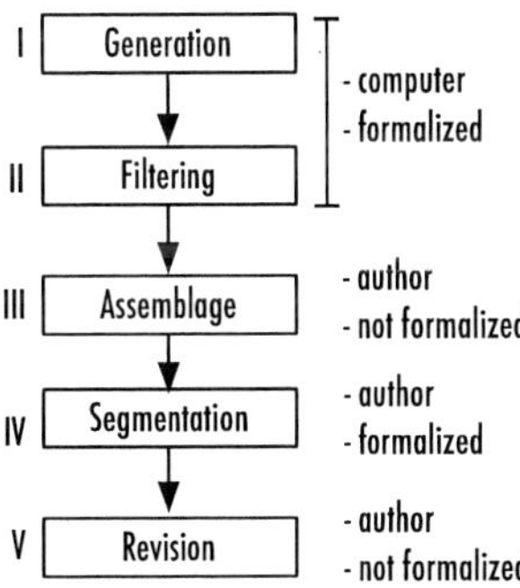

Figure 6: The conceptual schema of the *Tape Mark I* artwork

a permutation of the 15 fragments (provided by the programmer) and computes a specific combination. This means that the algorithm follows a brute-force approach, without any notion of valid sequence. In step II ("Filtering"), the computer removes the combinations that do not respect the rules expressed by the high-level algorithm. Step III is dedicated to the assemblage of valid sequences. The previously reconstructed methodology, strongly constrained by memory allocation techniques on the IBM 7070 and by AUTOCODER specifications, makes clear that the whole poem cannot be generated in one single run of the program, as the single run outputs a 10-element sequence. Thus, the poem is an assemblage of various outputs, an operation executed by Balestrini, that selects a number of combinations to be used together to produce the final opera[3]. In step IV ("Segmentation"), the author segments the combination in order to respect the chosen metrical constraints, i.e. 6 stanzas of 6 verses; In step V ("Revision"), the author adjusts a number of words in order to satisfy morphosyntactic constraints in the final text (e.g. verb-subject and number agreement).

One of the main goals of this paper is to understand the effort of the author, in other words what is the contribution of the poet in the *Tape Mark I* "electronic poem" (as computer-based poetry was called at times).

The most unclear point in the Balestrini's work is step I. Indeed, this step consists of two sub-processes: I-a) generate one permutation P of the 15 elements among the 15! possible permutations (1.307.674.368.000); I-b) generate all the possible combinations of 10 elements from P (i.e. without repetitions and permutations (Mazur, 2010)): for each P there are 3003 ($C(15:10)$ where C is the binomial coefficient) possible combinations[4].

The total number of possible outputs of *Tape Mark I*'s step I is huge: $P(15) * C(15:10) =$ 3,926,946,127,104,000. However, many of these sequences are identical, since the number of distinct sequences is $P(10) * C(15:10) =$

10,897,286,400. Finally, the total number of "valid" sequences, i.e. sequences respecting the constraints of instructions II and III, that we computed by generation and test, is 65,284,636.

One of the goals of the simulation is to understand how often the *Tape Mark I* was able to produce a valid sequence of fragments in output. So, we have implemented a program which reproduces the steps I and II of the flowchart in Figure 6. The original *Tape Mark I* program was able to generate the 3003 possible combinations of a single permutation in 660 seconds on the IBM 7070. We have implemented an optimized version of the same process by using C++: this program runs in 0.01 seconds on a modern laptop (4GB ram, i7 2GHz processor) to generate and test the 3003 possible combinations of a single permutation.[5] However, also with this fast program, we would need 414 years to test all the possible 15! permutations. So we decided to perform an experiment on ten millions random permutations of the 15 elements: for each permutation, we counted how many of the 3003 combinations were valid, i.e. how many combinations satisfy the constraints expressed in the high-level model. In this way, we can figure how often the original program produced an output that the poet could modify in the steps III and IV and V of Figure 6.

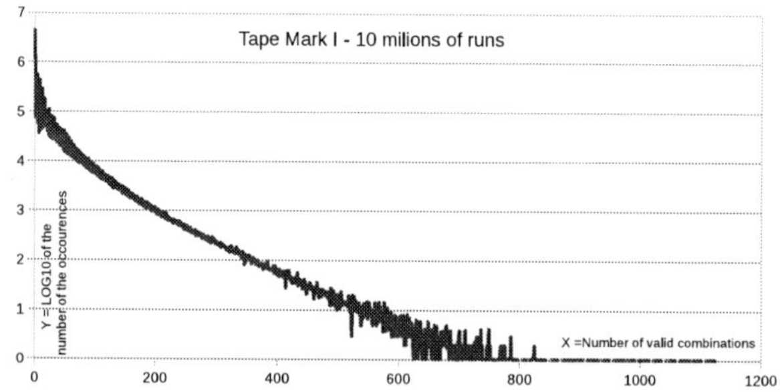

Figure 7: The number of occurrences of valid combinations found in 10 millions random permutations of the 15 elements.

We found that statistically half of the times all the 3003 combinations extracted from a permutation do not satisfy the required constraints. However, we also found that the maximum number of valid combinations from one single permutation was 1126 (see the logarithmic graph in Figure 7). So, this simula-

---

[3]This is evident in the poem by comparing the final verse of first stanza with the initial verse of the second one. They both belong to the same group (II), so the non-adjacent constraint of instruction II does not apply, as they are generated from two runs.

[4](Balestrini, 1962) incorrectly reports 3002.

[5]A first, non optimized version was implemented in Clojure and required 0.1 seconds.

tion confirms that in order to produce *Tape Mark I* the poet needed to run the program several times, adopting a severe trial and test procedure. Figure 8 shows an excerpt of the raw output of the system once printed on paper[6]. Three outputs of 10 elements are shown, the one on top is annotated to allow the reader to follow the chaining mechanism based on head and tail codes.

6 Balestrini vs computational creativity

In the light of the archaeological focus of our contribution we will not directly question the notion of computational creativity, rather we will discuss some aspects of Balestrini's work in relation to his computational practice and its critical reception. That is, we will address the question: what is (*ante litteram*) computational creativity for Balestrini in the Neo-avantgarde context of the '60s? In the following we identify some key features.

Formalization and metalanguage: a metalinguistic tension is a defining element in Balestrini's work, as content is subordinate to the explicit operations at the basis of its generation. The second poem collection by Balestrini is titled *Come si agisce* ("How to act") and its final section is a table that precisely specifies how the poems in the collection were created, and thus how to possibly create other, new poems: thus, "poetry is an operation, the poet shows, precisely, how to act" (Brancaleoni, 2007, 125). Not by chance, *Tape Mark I* has been overtly described in the *Almanacco*. To formalize the poetic operation -as noted by Sanguineti, poet but also prominent critic of the avantgarde- the use of the computer is in some sense a natural consequence of such an aesthetics: "electronic poetry is [...] the natural extreme outcome" of a similar aesthetics (Sanguineti, 1965, 72)[7]; **Materiality of language:** language, primarily on its expressive surface, and secondarily in relation to the conveyed content, is the matter of poetry. The poetry is intended on the one hand to demystify language by suspending its actual practicality, on the

other hand to drastically destroy meaning, in order to reach Barthes' "Degree Zero" of language, the level of its materiality (Brancaleoni, 2007). Computers allow to directly target this goal by efficiently providing symbol manipulation;

Redefinition of the role of the reader: thanks to digital printing, in the new Italian and English editions of Balestrini's novel *Tristano* (2015-16) (Balestrini, 2015; Balestrini, 2016), each copy is different from any other, thus reaching his original purpose, i.e. to escape "the rigid determinism of the mechanical Gutenberg printing process" (Balestrini, 2015). In the preface of the novel, Eco has individuated three radically different "roles of the reader" (Eco, 1984) implied in such a literary device, that indeed are at stake also in the case of *Tape Mark I*.

1. pick up a copy and read it as if it were original and unchangeable;
2. find multiple copies and retrace the different outcomes of combinatorics;
3. choose one among the many texts on the basis of the reader's evaluation criteria (Balestrini, 2015).

Such a dispersion of roles is possible only in case of usage of computer-controlled generative processes;

System vs text as a value for the open work: while poetry is typically placed at the text level, in Balestrini's approach it is the (generative) system at its origin that is considered in itself as a value, as the project is to undermine the dogma of the original, unique and definitive literary work. As noted by Eco, "the whole work resides in its variations, even in its variability. The electronic brain has made an attempt to create an *open work*" (Eco, 1962, 185)[8]. Hence the relevance of permutation, made possible only by computational means, as an exhaustive deployment of all the possible outcomes. Another historical example of such a permutative fury is Queneau's *Cent mille milliards de poèmes*, that was published exactly in the same year of Balestrini's *Tape Mark I*. Queneau, one of the founders of Oulipo, devised a typographical setting in which each sheet was cut into stripes. By turning the stripes, new poems emerge from the combinations of various lay-

---

[6]Initially, generated data were stored on magnetic tape, hence the name of the work. The final print was on a 63.74 meter continuous roll (Morando, 1962).

[7]Interestingly, (Colton et al., 2014) argue the relevance for the user to meta-linguistically document computational creative processes.

[8]Here Eco is referring to his notion of "open work" as a system of interpretative possibilities, that was originally published exactly in 1962 (Eco, 1989).

```
|MENTRE LA MOLTITUDINE |||1 DELLE COSE     ACCADE |  I  CAPELLI ||2  TRA LE LABBRA |TRENTA VOLTE |3 PIU
LUMINOSO  DEL SOLE | GIACQUERO ||3  IMMOBILI  SENZA PARLARE | MALGRADO  CHE LE COSE |||3 FIORISCANO |
SI  ESPANDE |2  RAPIDAMENTE | FINCHE NON MOSSE||3  LE DITA  LENTAMENTE  |  L ACCECANTE ||  GLOBO
DI FUOCO |CERCAND0|||4DI AFFERRARE | LA  SOMMITA |5 DELLA NUVOLA |

 MENTRE LA MOLTITUDINE     DELLE COSE      ACCADE    I  CAPELLI      TRA LE LABBRA  ESSE TORNANO   TUTT
E     ALLA LORO RADICE      L ACCECANTE      GLOBO    DI FUOCO   GIACQUERO     IMMOBILI  SENZA PARLARE
 TRENTA VOLTE    PIU LUMINOSO   DEL SOLE  FINCHE NON MOSSE   LE DITA   LENTAMENTE     SI  ESPANDE
  RAPIDAMENTE   CERCANDO  DI AFFERRARE   LA  SOMMITA    DELLA NUVOLA

 MENTRE LA MOLTITUDINE     DELLE COSE     ACCADE   L ACCECANTE      GLOBO    DI FUOCO  ESSE TORNANO
  TUTTE     ALLA LORO RADICE    SI  ESPANDE    RAPIDAMENTE   FINCHE NON MOSSE    LE DITA   LENTAMENT
E    QUANDO  RAGGIUNGE  LA STRATOSFERA   GIACQUERO     IMMOBILI  SENZA PARLARE  TRENTA VOLTE    PIU
LUMINOSO   DEL SOLE  CERCANDO  DI AFFERRARE    ASSUME   LA BEN NOTA FORMA   DI FUNGO
```

Figure 8: An excerpt of the raw output (four 10 element runs). On top, an annotated sequence showing the group and relative element index.

ers. It is interesting to note that Queneau aimed at creating "une sorte de machine à fabriquer des poèmes" (Queneau, 1961).

Poet as a distributed demiurge: as noted by Sanguineti, "the divine fury of the poet [...] is converted into the infinite technical possibilities of the electronic instrument, elected both as the imaginative stimulus and as the practical manufacturer" (Sanguineti, 1965, 75). Hence the subject gains a role of mediator, and it is distributed at various levels, in a shared association with machine's symbolic agency. Subjectivity thus emerges:

- in the choice of materials, both in terms of the source texts and their cutup;
- at the syntactic level (the definition of the grammar, even if the term does not properly apply);
- in the selection and assemblage of the outputs and in the final revision (punctuation and syntactic agreement)[9].

To sum up, it is worth emphasizing again Sanguineti's observation: computational poetry is the natural extreme outcome of such an aesthetics. In the case of *Tape Mark I* creativity is intrinsically computational as it is intrinsically shared between man and the machine.

7 Conclusions

Our aim was to inspect into details a substantially well documented example of computer-generated poetry. A first interesting result is that low-level features, that depends on available technology at a certain historical time, have a crucial impact on the output, as evident in the friction, so to say, between high- and low-level algorithms. Is *Tape Mark I* a good example of computer-generated poem? The answer to this question is simply yes, as *Tape Mark I*, far from being an experiment, is a crucial case, highly considered in literature (hence, its interest). And, thus, can the operations at its basis be considered relevant for a general model of computer poetry? The procedures devised by Balestrini are intrinsically local to his aesthetic vision and to the historical context (including the technological one, as we discussed). In this sense, our study seems to suggest that, differently from natural language, the results of poetry (and of all aesthetic objects) must be assessed in relation to its *Wirkungsgeschichte* (Gadamer, 2004), that is, the history of its effects on a certain community.

References

Oscar Alicicco, Laura Mastroddi, and Federica Romanò, editors. 2010. *I novissimi. Ricostruzione del fenomeno editoriale*. Oblique Studio, Roma.

Nanni Balestrini. 1962. Tape Mark I. In Sergio Morando, editor, *Almanacco letterario Bompiani 1962: le applicazioni dei calcolatori elettronici alle scienze morali e alla letteratura*. Bompiani.

Nanni Balestrini. 1968. Tape Mark I. In J. Reichardt, editor, *Cybernetic Serendipity: The Computer and the Arts : a Studio International Special Issue*, Studio international. Special issue. Studio International.

Nanni Balestrini. 2015. *Tristano*. DeriveApprodi, Roma.

Nanni Balestrini. 2016. *Tristano*. Verso, London –New York.

Margaret A. Boden. 2015. Foreword: How Computational Creativity Began. In Tarek R. Besold,

---

[9]In any case, Balestrini was positive on a future automatization of the Revision step (Morando, 1962).

Marco Schorlemmer, and Alan Smaill, editors, *Computational Creativity Research: Towards Creative Machines*, volume 7. Atlantis Press.

Claudio Brancaleoni, 2007. *Re-lab: immagini parole*, chapter "La rivoluzione in forma di parole": Nanni Balestrini, pages 125–136. Morlacchi, Perugia.

Simon Colton, Michael Cook, Rose Hepworth, and Alison Pease. 2014. On acid drops and teardrops: Observer issues in computational creativity. In *Proceedings of the 50th Anniversary Convention of the AISB*. Society for the Study of Artificial Intelligence and Simulation of Behaviour.

Adriano Comai. 1985. Poesie elettroniche. L'esempio di Balestrini. Master's thesis, Università di Torino, Torino.

Umberto Eco. 1962. La forma del disordine. In Sergio Morando, editor, *Almanacco letterario Bompiani 1962: le applicazioni dei calcolatori elettronici alle scienze morali e alla letteratura*, pages 175–188. Bompiani.

Umberto Eco. 1984. *The Role of the Reader*. Indiana UP, Bloomington.

Umberto Eco. 1989. *The Open Work*. Harvard UP, Cambridge, Mass.

Christopher T. Funkhouser and Sandy Baldwin. 2007. *Prehistoric Digital Poetry: An Archaeology of Forms, 1959-1995*. Modern & Contemporary Poetics. University of Alabama Press.

Hans-Georg Gadamer. 2004. *Truth and Method*. Continuum, New York.

Gervás, Pablo. 2015. Deconstructing Computer Poets: Making Selected Processes Available as Services. *Computational Intelligence*.

Pablo Gervas. 2016. Constrained creation of poetic forms during theme-driven exploration of a domain defined by an n-gram model. *Connection Science*, 28(2):111–130, April.

Alfredo Giuliani, editor. 1961. *I novissimi. Poesie per gli anni '60*. Rusconi e Paolazzi, Milano.

John E. Hopcroft, Rajeev Motwani, and Jeffrey D. Ullman. 2006. *Introduction to Automata Theory, Languages, and Computation (3rd Edition)*. Addison-Wesley Longman Publishing Co., Inc., Boston, MA, USA.

IBM. 1961. Reference manual ibm 7070 series programming systems autocoder. Technical report, IBM, New York.

Vincenzo Lombardo, Andrea Valle, Fabrizio Nunnari, Francesco Giordana, and Andrea Arghinenti. 2006. Archeology of multimedia. In *Proceedings of the 14th ACM International Conference on Multimedia*, MM '06, pages 269–278, New York, NY, USA. ACM.

Brent MacGregor. 2002. Cybernetic serendipity revisited. In *C&C '02: Proceedings of the 4th Conference on Creativity & Cognition*, pages 11–13, New York, NY, USA. ACM.

D.R. Mazur. 2010. *Combinatorics: A Guided Tour*. MAA textbooks. Mathematical Association of America.

Sergio Morando, editor. 1962. *Almanacco letterario Bompiani 1962: le applicazioni dei calcolatori elettronici alle scienze morali e alla letteratura*. Bompiani.

Raymond Queneau. 1961. *Cent mille milliards de poèmes*. Gallimard, Paris.

Jasia Reichardt, editor. 1968. *Cybernetic Serendipity. The computer and the arts*. Number Special Issue. Studio International, New York.

Ehud Reiter. 2007. An architecture for data-to-text systems. In *Proceedings of the Eleventh European Workshop on Natural Language Generation*, ENLG '07, pages 97–104, Stroudsburg, PA, USA. Association for Computational Linguistics.

Gian Paolo Renello. 2010. *Machinae. Studi sulla poetica di Nanni Balestrini,*. Il Castello di Atlante. Bologna, CLUEB.

Edoardo Sanguineti. 1965. *Ideologia e linguaggio*. Feltrinelli, Milano.

Jukka M. Toivanen, Hannu Toivonen, Alessandro Valitutti, and Oskar Gross. 2012. Corpus-based generation of content and form in poetry. In *Proceedings of the Third International Conference on Computational Creativity*, page 211–215, Dublin, Ireland, may.

La testa premuta sulla spalle, trenta volte
più luminoso del sole, io contemplo il loro ritorno
finché non mosse le dita lentamente e, mentre la moltitudine
delle cose accade, alla sommità della nuvola
esse tornano tutte, alla loro radice, e assumono
la ben nota forma di fungo cercando di afferrare.

Head pressed on shoulder, thirty times
brighter than the sun I envisage their return,
until he moved his fingers slowly and while the multitude
of things comes into being, at the summit of the cloud
they all return to their roots and take on
the well known mushroom shape endeavouring to grasp.

I capelli tra le labbra, esse tornano tutte
alla loro radice, nell'accecante globo di fuoco
io contemplo il loro ritorno, finché non muove le dita
lentamente, e malgrado che le cose fioriscano
assume la ben nota forma di fungo, cercando
di afferrare mente la moltitudine delle cose accade.

Hair between lips, they all return
to their roots, in the blinding fireball
I envisage their return, until he moves his fingers
slowly, and although things flourish
takes on the well known mushroom shape
endeavouring to grasp while the multitude of things comes into being.

Nell'accecante globo di fuoco io contemplo
il loro ritorno quando raggiunge la stratosfera mentre la moltitudine
delle cose accade, la testa premuta
sulla spalla: trenta volte più luminose del sole
esse tornano tutte alla loro radice, i capelli
tra le labbra assumono la ben nota forma di fungo.

In the blinding fireball I envisage
their return when it reaches the stratosphere while the multitude
of things comes into being, head pressed
on shoulder, thirty times brighter than the sun
they all return to their roots, hair
between lips takes on the well known mushroom shape.

Giacquero immobili senza parlare, trenta volte
più luminosi del sole essi tornano tutti
alla loro radice, la testa premuta sulla spalla
assumono la ben nota forma di fungo cercando
di afferrare, e malgrado che le cose fioriscano
si espandono rapidamente, i capelli tra le labbra.

They lay motionless without speaking, thirty times
brighter than the sun they all return
to their roots, head pressed on shoulder
they take on the well known mushroom shape endeavouring
to grasp, and although things flourish
they expand rapidly, hair between lips.

Mentre la moltitudine delle cose accade nell'accecante
globo di fuoco, esse tornano tutte
alla loro radice, si espandono rapidamente, finché non mosse
le dita lentamente quando raggiunse la stratosfera
e giacque immobile senza parlare, trenta volte
più luminoso del sole, cercando di afferrare.

While the multitude of things comes into being in the blinding
fireball, they all return
to their roots, they expand rapidly, until he moved
his fingers slowly when it reached the stratosphere
and lay motionless without speaking, thirty times
brighter than the sun endeavouring to grasp.

Io contemplo il loro ritorno, finché non mosse le dita
lentamente nell'accecante globo di fuoco:
esse tornano tutte alla loro radice, i capelli
tra le labbra e trenta volte più luminosi del sole
giacquero immobili senza parlare, si espandono
rapidamente cercando di afferrare la sommità.

I envisage their return, until he moved his fingers
slowly in the blinding fireball,
they all return to their roots, hair
between lips and thirty times brighter than the sun
lay motionless without speaking, they expand
rapidly endeavouring to grasp the summit.

Figure 9: *Tape Mark I.* The Italian original version and the English translation (from Balestrini, 1968).

Author Index

Association for Computational Linguistics
209 N. Eighth Street
Stroudsburg, Pennsylvania 18360

ISBN 978-1-5108-3184-1